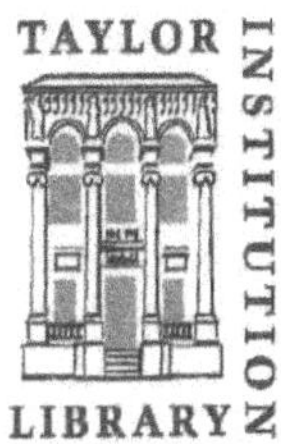

Treasures of the Taylorian:
Series Three: Cultural Memory
Volume 8

LOOKING for DANTE

Exploring the 'Divine Comedy' in Print from the 15th Century to Today

Wuon-Gean Ho, Rebecca Bowen

& Simon Gilson

Taylor Institution Library, Oxford, 2024

First published in 2024 by Taylor Institution Library

http://www.bodleian.ox.ac.uk/taylor

Cover images, front: *Dante – Touch In / In Touch* (2024) by Wuon-Gean Ho. Linocut and Monoprint, 20 x 15 cm. Back: *Dante – Gaza* (2024) by Wuon-Gean Ho. Linocut and Monoprint, 15 x 20 cm. Courtesy of the artist.

This project was funded by a TORCH Knowledge Exchange innovation Fund Award. It is affiliated to the ARHC project 'Envisioning Dante, c. 1472-c. 1630: Seeing and Reading the Early Printed Page'.

Typesetting and cover design by Arthur Bowen

Series editor: Henrike Lähnemann

ISBN 978-1-8384641-9-6

Taylor Institution Library, St Giles, Oxford, OX1 3NA

LOOKING *for* DANTE

Exploring the 'Divine Comedy' in Print from the 15th Century to Today

Wuon-Gean Ho, Rebecca Bowen
& Simon Gilson

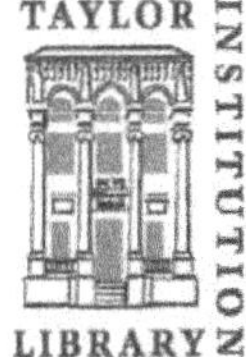

Table of Contents

List of Figures

Preface

Looking for Dante

When we pick up a book, we often forget that as well as reading a text we are looking at an object. Unlike the relative intangibility of words, which dwell in our minds and memories as well as on the page, screen, or writing surface before us, books are things – they have a physical presence in the world and a material history to go along with it. Some books call out to be seen, maximising their visual appeal with images or interesting layouts. This is certainly the case for Dante's medieval masterwork, the *Commedia*, known as the 'Divine Comedy' in English. Written in the early 1300s, Dante's poem is an intensely envisioned journey through the three realms of the Christian afterlife (Inferno, Purgatory, and Paradise). The poem was the subject of vivid illustrations and, when book making transitioned into the new medium of print in the late 1400s, it inspired new visual traditions.

Seeking to see some of these early printed Dantes in more detail and to explore the meanings they can still hold for us today, Simon Gilson and I – two University of Oxford specialists in Dante Studies and Book History – invited the artist and printmaker Wuon-Gean Ho to examine and respond to historical editions of the *Divine Comedy* held in the special collections of the University of Oxford's Taylor Institution Library. These holdings are astonishing, stretching across the first 150 years of printing, from the experimentations of the late 1400s to the elaborate designs of the sixteenth century. Through a series of encounters in the archive, we exchanged ideas about the history and content of these renaissance books as well as the material and artistic processes that brought them into being.

'Looking for Dante' is the result of this journey through the afterlife of the *Divine Comedy* in print, from the imagined spaces of Dante's poem and the historical books the preserve it to the physical spaces of the Taylor Library and the printshop that still operates today in the Old Bodleian Library, where Wuon-Gean inked and printed a new series of prints, presented in Part I of this catalogue. An embodied response to the poem as well as the archives and library spaces that conserve it, the 'Looking for Dante' print series immerse us in Wuon-Gean's experience as a reader. Across these prints, the poem takes root in her imagination, moves from the pages of the early printed books onto those of her sketch book and then spills out into the library, offering a modern reading of Dante captured in the same artistic medium that, since the late 1400s, has preserved the poem to this day: print. These artworks, which include a series of prints and a short film, are presented alongside lines from Dante's poem and reflections on the artist's process.

Turning to the collaborative process and the historical books that inspired it, Part II presents essays by the project's contributors. Wuon-Gean reflects on her encounters as a printmaker with editions in the Taylorian special collections and in her essay opens a window onto the project as it unfolded. Turning to the books in the archive, Simon Gilson offers insight into the panorama of printing the *Divine Comedy* in the fifteenth and sixteenth centuries, while the last essay explores the illustrations developed for these early printed books and discusses their points of connection with Wuon-Gean's new prints.

This project was funded by a TORCH Knowledge Exchange Innovation Fund Award. It is part of the AHRC Project 'Envisioning Dante, c. 1472-c. 1630: Seeing and Reading the Early Printed Page', led by Professor Guyda Armstrong at the University of Manchester. The grant holders would like to thank Richard Lawrence and Alexandra Franklin at the Bodleian, and the staff at the Taylor Institution Library, especially Andrea Del Cornò, Joanne Ferrari, Emma Huber, and Frank Egerton.

Passages from *Inferno* and *Purgatory* are quoted from the translation by Dorothy L. Sayers, *The Comedy of Dante Alighieri, the Florentine* (Penguin Books). Passages from *Paradise* are cited from the translation by Henry Wadsworth Longfellow, *The Divine Comedy of Dante Alighieri* (Ticknor and Fields) .

Looking for Dante: Part I

Dante – Camera (2024) by Wuon-Gean Ho. Linocut and Monoprint, 20 x 15 cm.

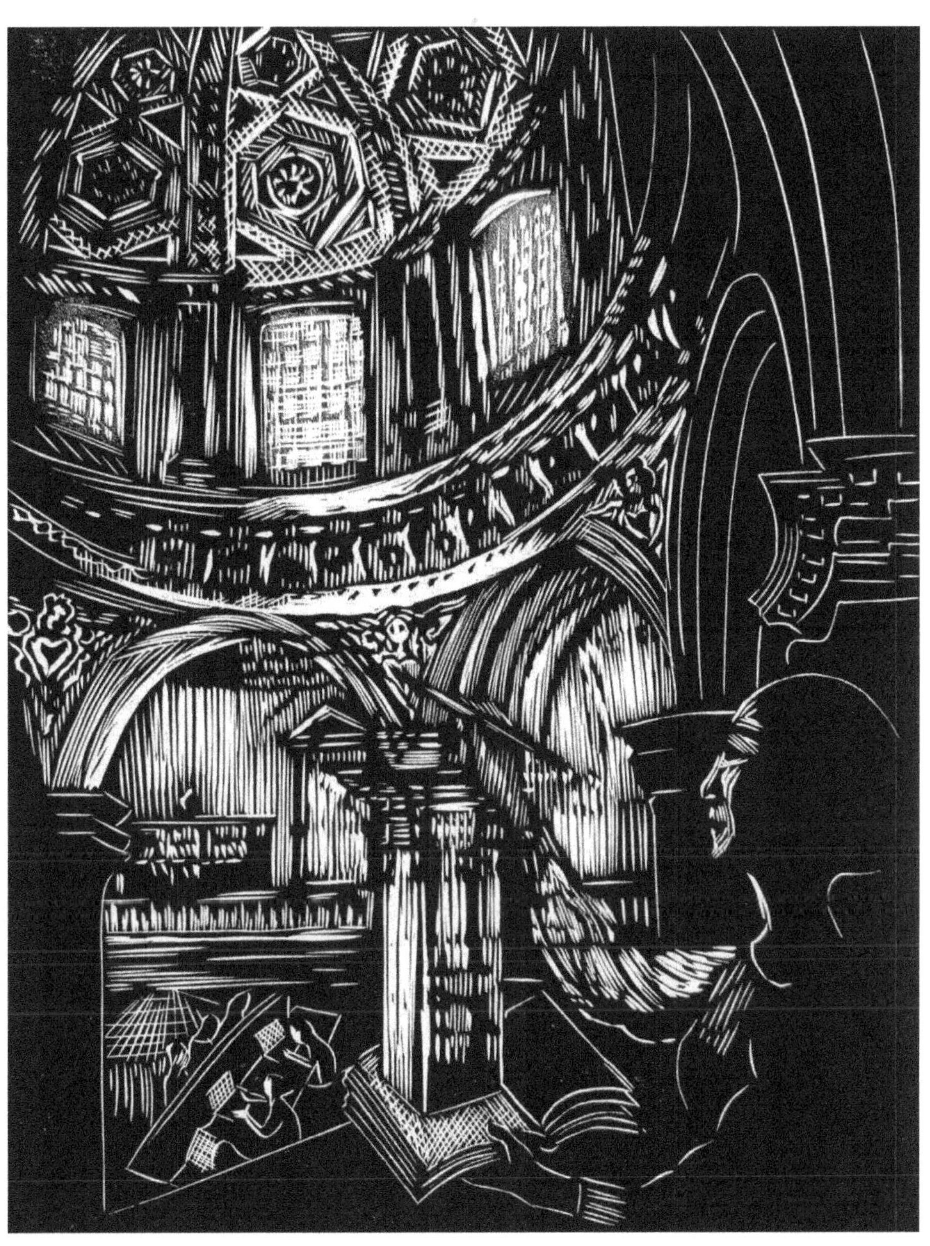

If the world were arranged
in the order which I see in yonder wheels,
what's set before me would have satisfied me (...)

in this miraculous and angelic temple,
that has for confines only love and light.

Paradise 28.46–57

Dante - Camera is a print about the act of authorship: the act of creating a space and telling a story within the pages of a book. A lofty domed space, inspired by the famous Oxford building called the Radcliffe Camera, appears to spring from the artist's sketchbook. The walls and pillars are in the process of being drawn by a brush held in the artist's hand. The print comments on the notion of creating a believable miniature world for fantastical stories to occur, a notion which is also true for the *Divine Comedy*.

WGH

When he is almost at the top of Paradise, Dante encounters the angels arranged in circles that wheel up far above him, beautiful and almost overwhelming. In *Dante - Camera*, Wuon-Gean is also looking up as the domed ceiling of the Radcliffe Camera springs to life before her. The figures in between the arches at the bottom of the scene could be praying, but they are probably using their laptops like most of the people who come to this library which is a temple to reading rather than religion.

RB

Overleaf: *Dante – Shield* (2024) by Wuon-Gean Ho.
Linocut and Monoprint, 15 x 20 cm.

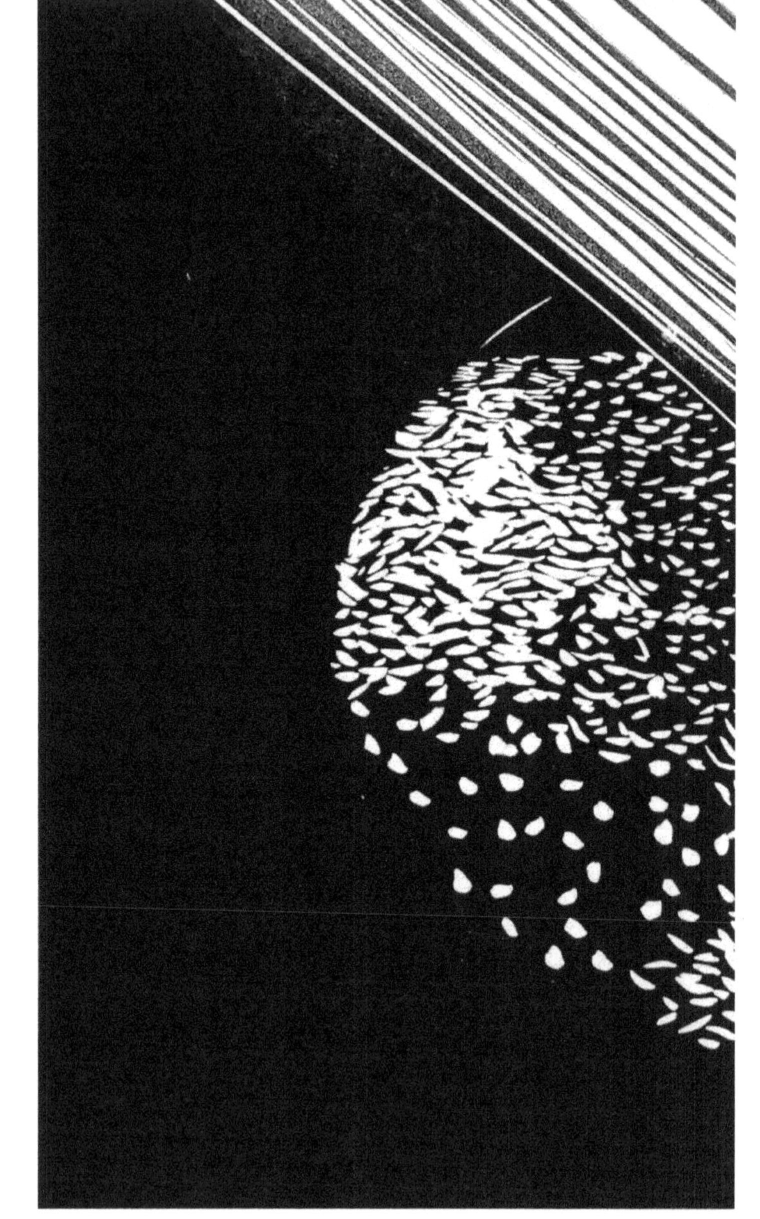

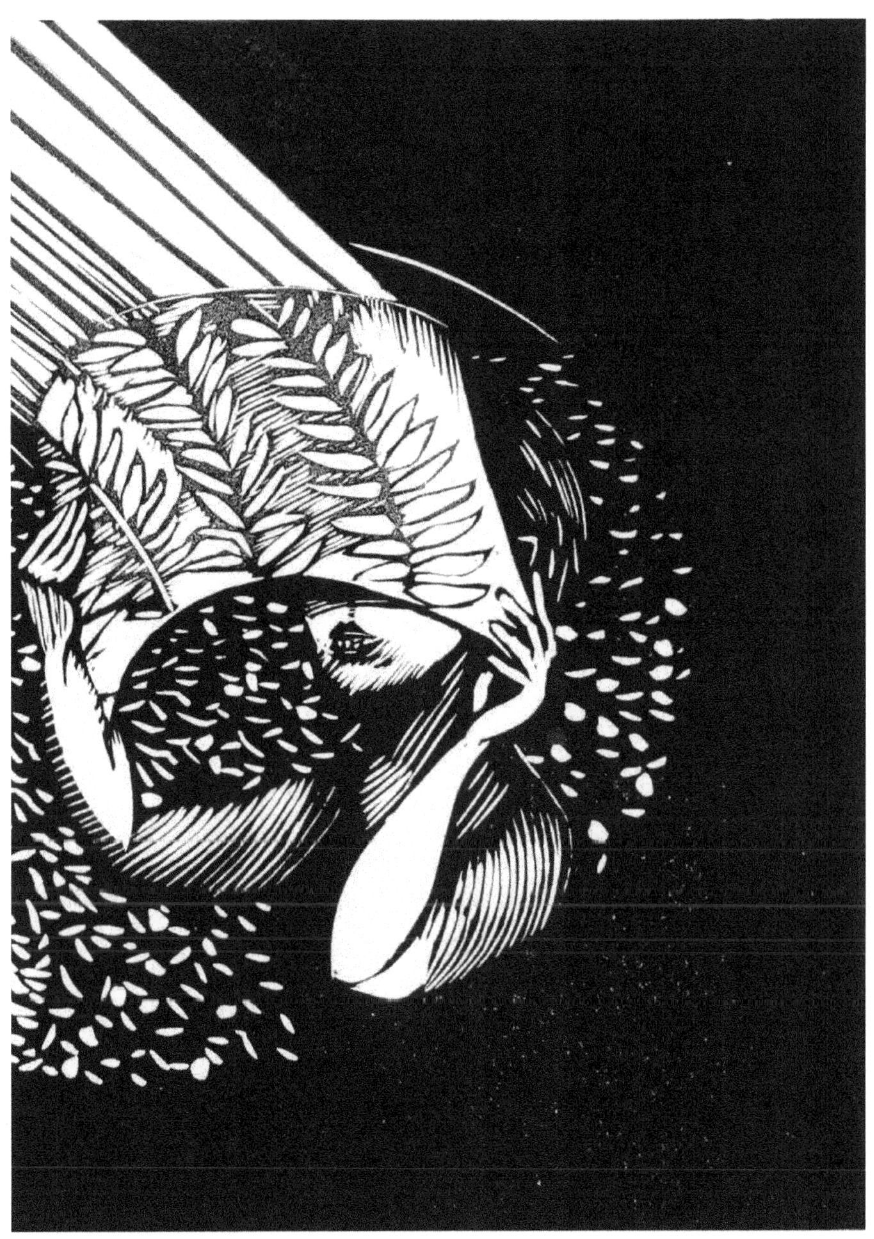

Lift up then, Reader, to the lofty wheels
with me thy vision straight unto that part
where the one motion on the other strikes,

and there begin to contemplate with joy
that Master's art, who in himself so loves it
that never does his eye from it depart.

Paradise 10.7–12

Dante - Shield is a print about Dante seeking the heavens but being dazzled by the light of knowledge. The shield is embossed with a laurel wreath, a connection used in the early printed books to signify Dante's achievements as a poet. An attempt at engaging with old texts could be seen as an attempt at throwing light on the past. After the image was completed, a larger colour version was made upon witnessing the solar eclipse in April 2024. The tangible nature of the light of the sun is conveyed through the obvious traces of touch used in making the final image.

WGH

Books can be portals into other worlds. Dante knew this and encourages his readers to recognise it by directly addressing us at several points in his poem, drawing our attention to his descriptions but also reminding us of the book in our hands. *Dante - Shield* has a similar effect, encouraging us to think about the experience of 'seeing' a story, while foregrounding the page that is the medium of that vision and the ink without which it would be blank.

RB

Overleaf: Dante – *Am-Or / Am-More* (2024) by Wuon-Gean Ho.
Linocut and Monoprint, 15 x 20 cm.

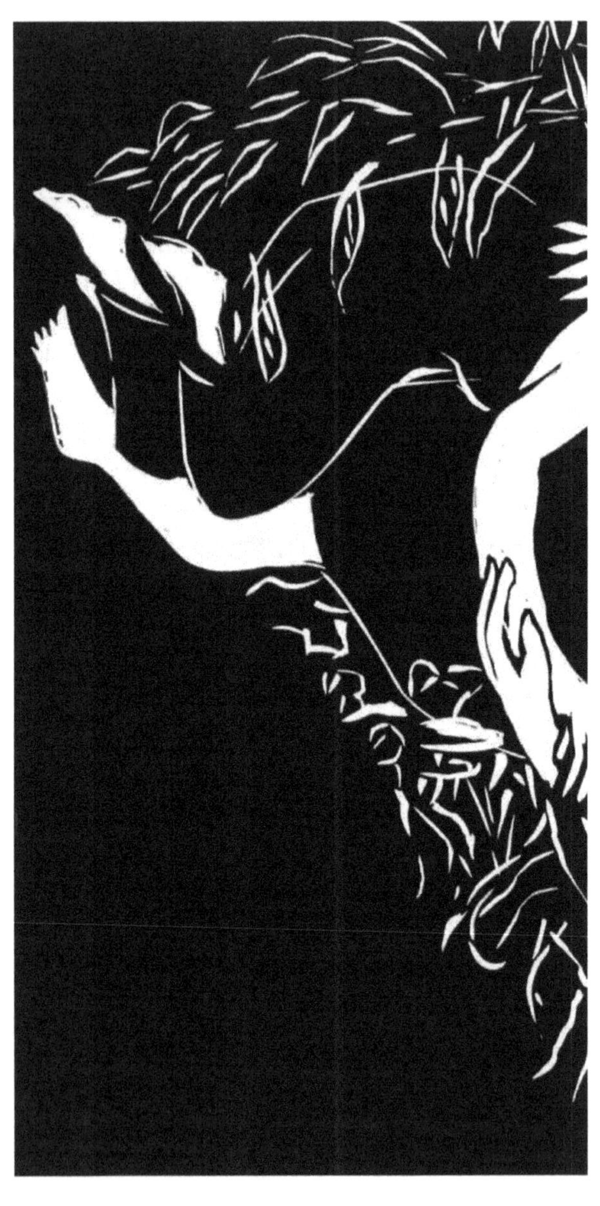

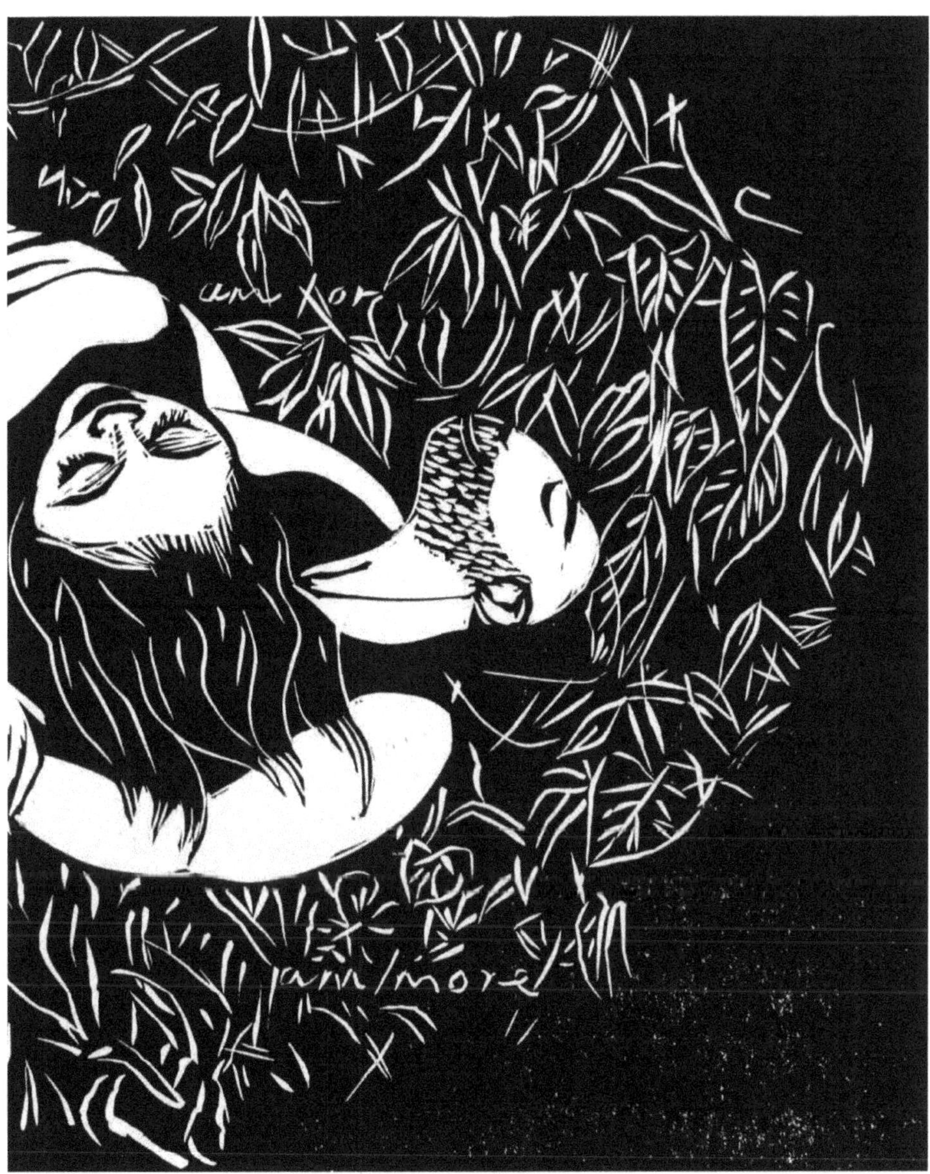
am for
am/more

Amor, ch'al cor gentil ratto s'apprende,
prese costui de la bella persona
che mi fu tolta; e 'l modo ancor m'offende.

Amor, ch'a nullo amato amar perdona,
mi prese del costui piacer sì forte,
che, come vedi, ancor non m'abbandona.

Amor condusse noi ad una morte.

Love, that so soon takes hold in the gentle breast.
Took this lad with the lovely body they tore
from me; the way of it leaves me still distrest.

Love, that to no loved heart remits love's score,
took me with such great joy of him, that see!
It holds me yet and never shall leave me more.

Love to a single death brought him and me.

Inferno 5.100–106

Dante - Am-Or / Am-More. This print is a pun on the wordplay of the Italian word *amore*. In English "a-m-o-r-e" can be combined to form words which reflect on the transitional aspect of relationships and entanglement. This could be read for example as an invitation between optional identities to become more. Dante's Italian, which refers to Paolo and Francesca's short affair, plays upon the similarity of the word "amore" to "a morte", or "love" "to death". The carving of the foliage is a visual commentary on the virtuoso carving of the foliage in the woodcuts included in the edition printed by Marcolini in 1544. As woodcuts are relief prints, it is necessary to carve everything away which will not print. In other words, in order to make an image appear like a brush drawing, both sides of the dark brushstroke must be carved away on the block. Instead of attempting this labour, the drawing is rendered as a white line against a dark background.

WGH

When Dante meets the lovers Francesca and Paolo in the fifth circle of Hell, Francesca silences the infernal winds that rage around her and speaks so beautifully about the affair that landed her in trouble that Dante is overcome with pity and faints at the end of her speech. The print *Dante - Am-Or / Am-More* captures a 'tempo felice' (happy time) like the one that Francesca speaks about, but it also alludes to a darker side of love in which the lovers' embrace is an infernal punishment, not a heavenly reward.

RB

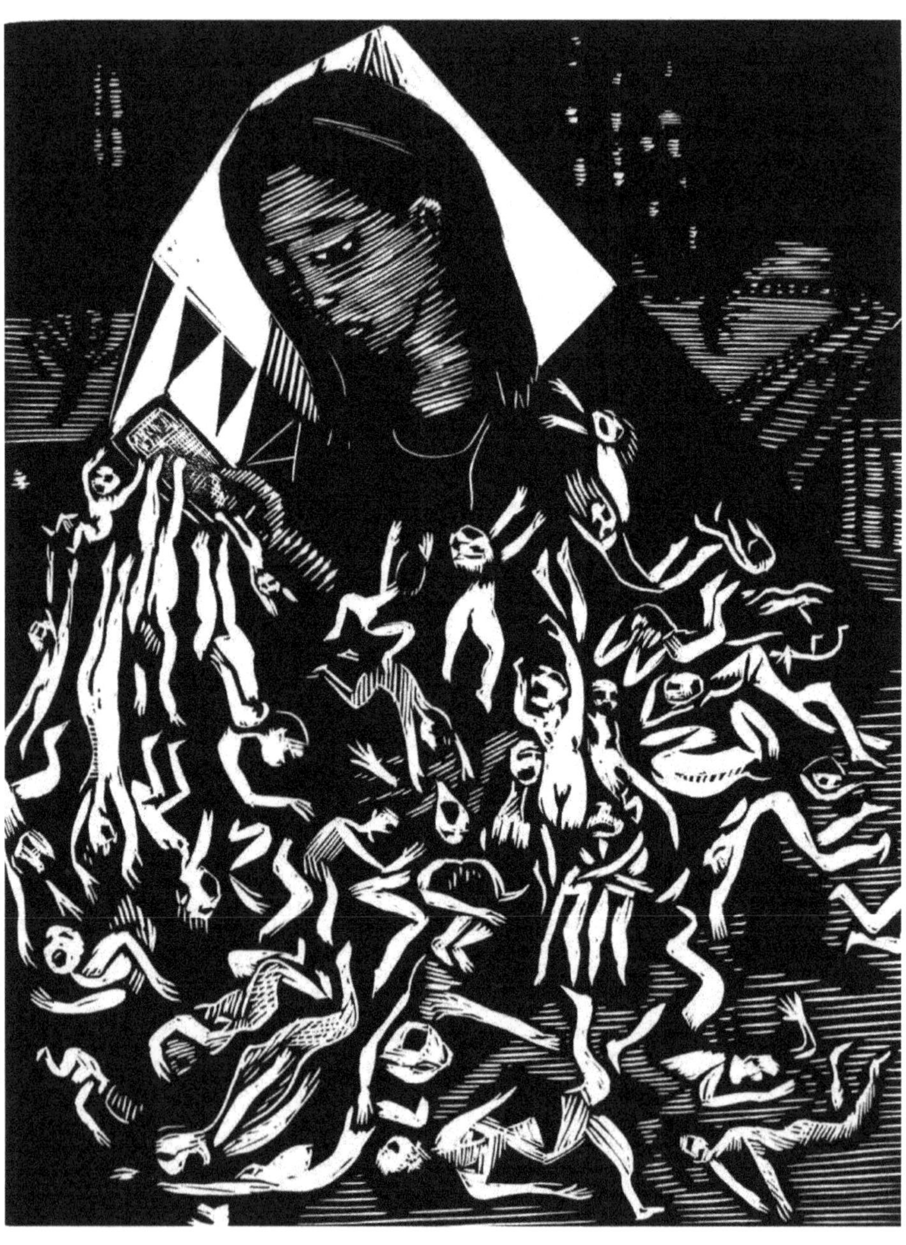

Dante – It Spills from the Screen (2024) by Wuon-Gean Ho.
Linocut and Monoprint, 20 x 15 cm

Then I: "But, Master, by what torment spurred
are they driven on to vent such bitter breath?"
He answered: "I will tell thee in a word:

this dreary huddle has no hope of death,
yet its blind life trails on so low and crass
that every other fate it envieth.

No reputation in the world it has,
mercy and doom hold it alike in scorn
let us not speak of these; but look, and pass."

Inferno 3.43–51

Dante - It Spills from the Screen. Images of specific scenes in the *Divine Comedy* such as the frozen lake of hell hold little resonance in the current day. In contrast, the close graphic nature of news reportage, as communicated through the phone screen, force a state of witnessing and engagement that might be compared to the impact of early printed books. *It Spills from the Screen* is a print about witnessing horrors that spill from the pocket held device, in much the same way as these early printed texts may also have conveyed the horrors of hell to the reader.

WGH

Dante - It Spills from the Screen turns the modern medium of the mobile phone into a page-like window through which images of human suffering pour out into the world. Like the mass of bodies described by Dante in *Inferno*, the figures in this print become a tangle of limbs under the artist's gaze. By making himself a character in his poem, Dante reflects on the scenes that he brings before his readers' eyes, some of which – like the conversation in Limbo quoted on the facing page – he does not try to explain.

RB

Overleaf: *Dante – Lamentation* (2024) by Wuon-Gean Ho.
Linocut and Monoprint, 15 x 20 cm.

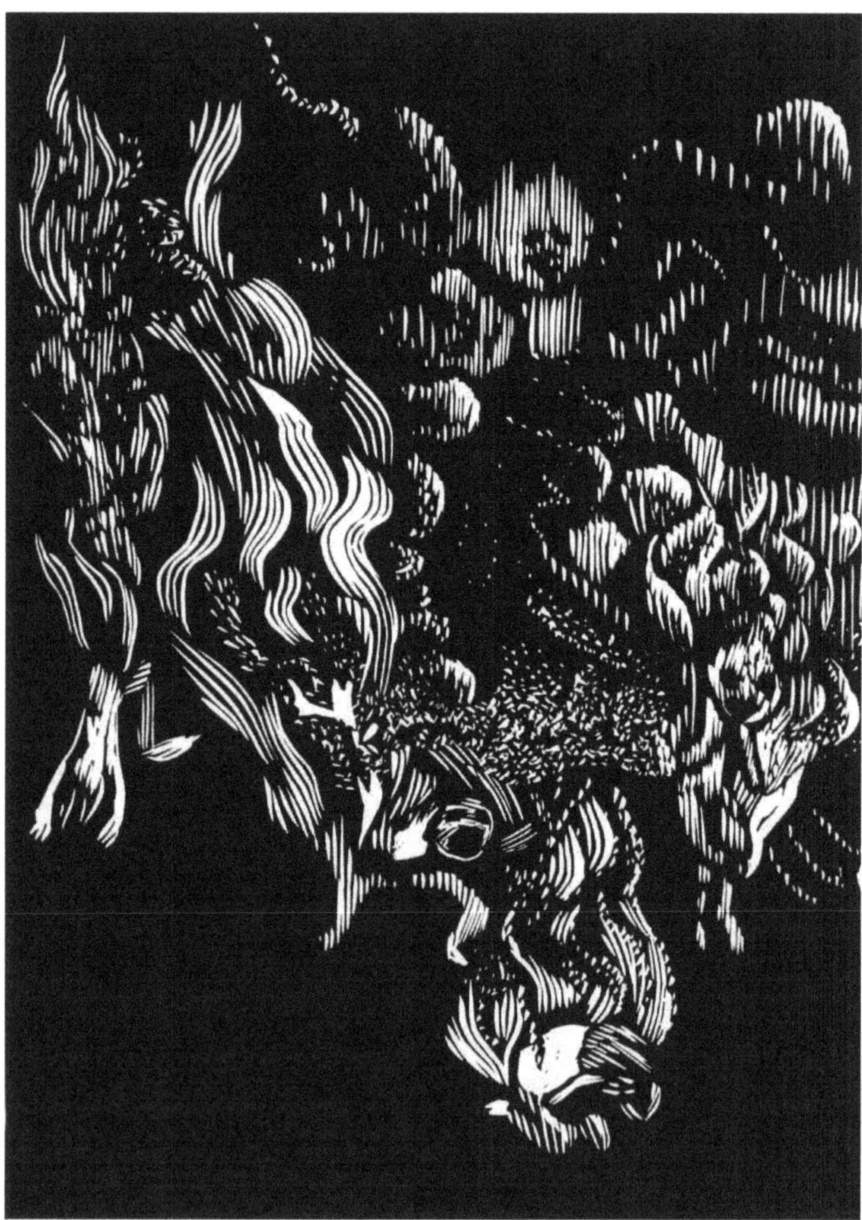

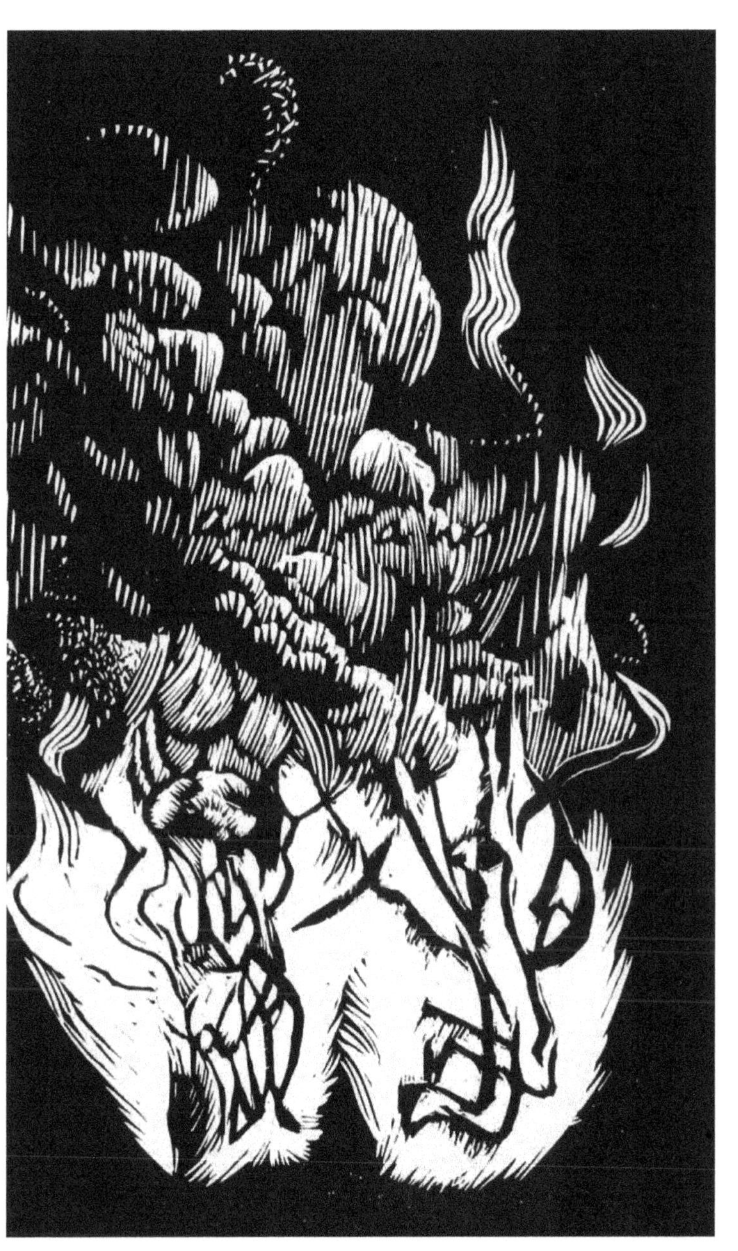

Then I: "O Master! If these sparks have skill
to speak, I pray, and re-pray that each prayer
may count with thee for prayers innumerable.

Deny me not to tarry a moment here
until the horned flame come; how much I long
and lean to it I think thee well aware." (...)

Then of that age-old fire the loftier horn
began to mutter and move, as a wavering flame
wrestles against the wind and is over-worn;

And, like a speaking tongue vibrant to frame
language, the tip of it flickering to and fro
threw out a voice and answered.

Inferno 26.79–84; 85–90

Dante - Lamentation is a print about the sacrifice of innocents as collateral damage in conflict zones, specifically about the burning of olive groves in the West Bank. The trees are populated with beings, who cry as they burn. Continuing on the concept of word-play on the word "amore" in this print, hidden in the scene, are the words "am-raw/am-war".

WGH

Deep in hell Dante encounters a circle of sinners trapped inside flames. As well as being shocked by the sight, he is drawn to the souls being punished and begs to talk to them. Multiple souls are held inside these fires, making the punishment intimate as well as isolating. The sinner who speaks to Dante is Ulysses, the protagonist of Homer's ancient epic poem and a man who supposedly sailed to the ends of the earth before ending up in *Inferno*. The parallel that Wuon-Gean draws with contemporary conflicts presents a chilling counterpart to Dante's imagined scene: the flames in this print do not hold literary characters.

RB

Overleaf: *Dante – Gaza* (2024) by Wuon-Gean Ho.
Linocut and Monoprint, 15 x 20 cm.

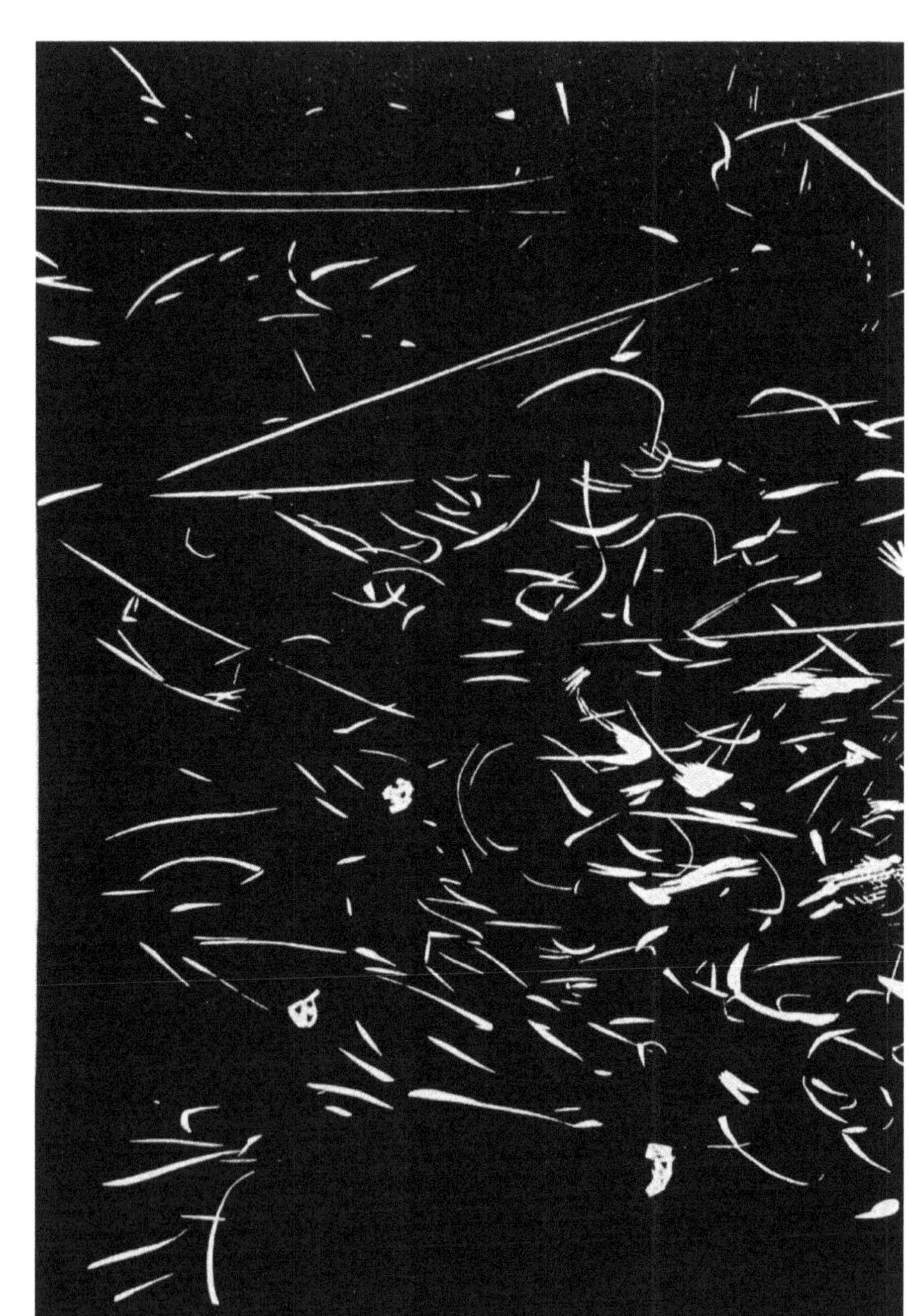

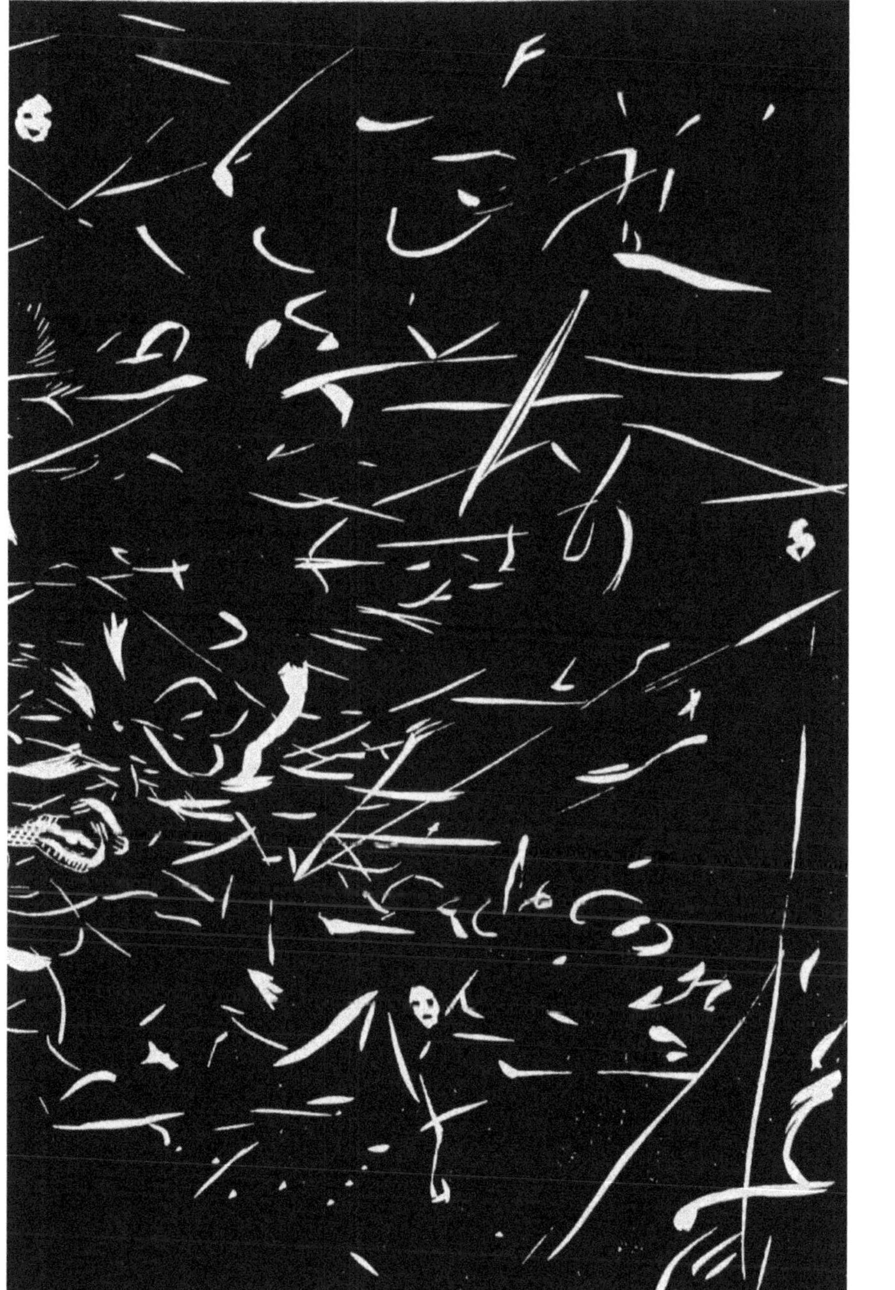

And now the sounds of grief begin to fill
My ear; I'm come where cries of anguish smite
My shrinking sense, and lamentation shrill –

A place made dumb of every glimmer of light,
Which bellows like tempestuous ocean birling
In the batter of a two-way wind's buffet and fight.

The blast of hell that never rests from whirling
Harries the spirits along in the sweep of its swath,
And vexes them, for ever beating and hurling.

When they are borne to the rim of the ruinous path
With cry, wail and shriek they are caught by the gust.

Inferno 5.25–35

Dante - Gaza. This print was made while observing war footage of explosions and how bodies and buildings become dust.

WGH

Early in *Inferno* Dante describes a storm that hurls the souls around and never lets them rest. Their laments are caught on this wind, as well as their shadowy bodies. Here, Dante uses soundscape to produce a sense of fragmentation while in Wuon-Gean's print scraps of white tear through the dark ink showing the page beneath.

RB

Dante – Touch In / In Touch (2024) by Wuon-Gean Ho. Linocut, 20 x 15 cm.

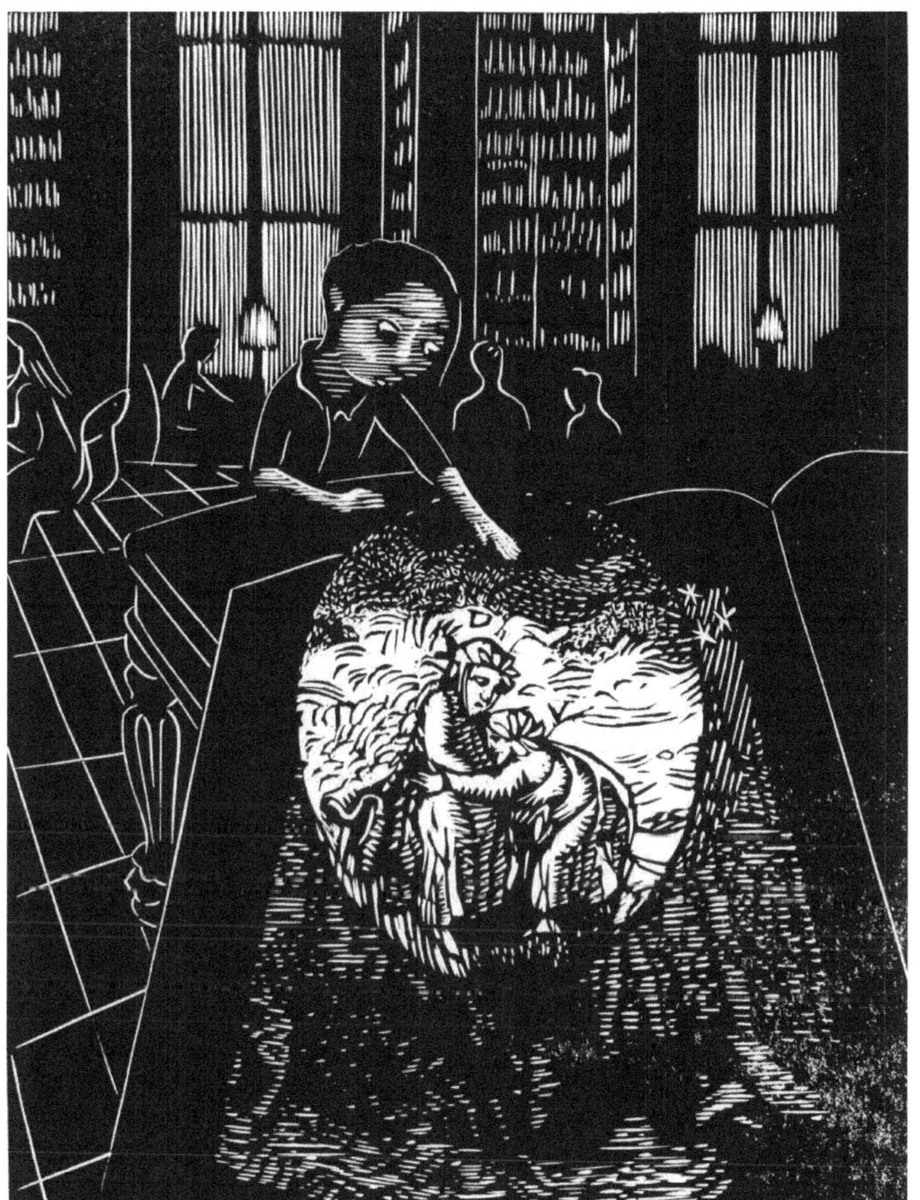

How should I go there? Who says so? Why?
I'm not Aeneas, and I am not Paul!
Who thinks me fit? Not others. And not I.

Say I submit, and go – suppose I fall
into some folly? Though I speak but ill,
thy better wisdom will construe it all."

As one who wills, and then unwills his will,
changing his mind with every changing whim,
till all his best intentions come to nil.

So I stood havering in that moorland dim.
While through fond rifts of fancy oozed away
the first quick zest that filled me to the brim.

Inferno 2.31–42

Dante - Touch In / In Touch is a rendition of a scene in the edition of the *Comedia* printed by Marcolini in 1544 where Virgil grasps Dante's waist. The mountain of Purgatory is in the distance and water and grass are in the foreground. The characters have the labels D and V over their heads. As blocks are reversed upon printing, the image in this print is a mirror of that in the text. The artist-as-researcher sits at the top of the image, extending a soft hand out to bridge the divide of time. The past is inside an egg: fragile, horizon-less, with potential. The scene is set in the Taylorian Institute, a beautiful Oxford library, where, despite the potential to engage with books and paper, most students sit in front of their screens.

WGH

At the start of *Inferno*, Dante is reluctant to journey into hell and asks his guide, Virgil, whether he is really the right man for the trip. As on many other occasions in the poem, Virgil's reassurance is enough to encourage him to continue his journey. Although this print shows a scene from the start of Purgatory, when Virgil helps Dante to complete a number of purifying rites (including tying a reed around his waist – the same gesture seen in this image), there is a hesitancy that recalls Dante's first moment of doubt as the reader comes into touch with the book that allows her to journey into Dante's poem.

RB

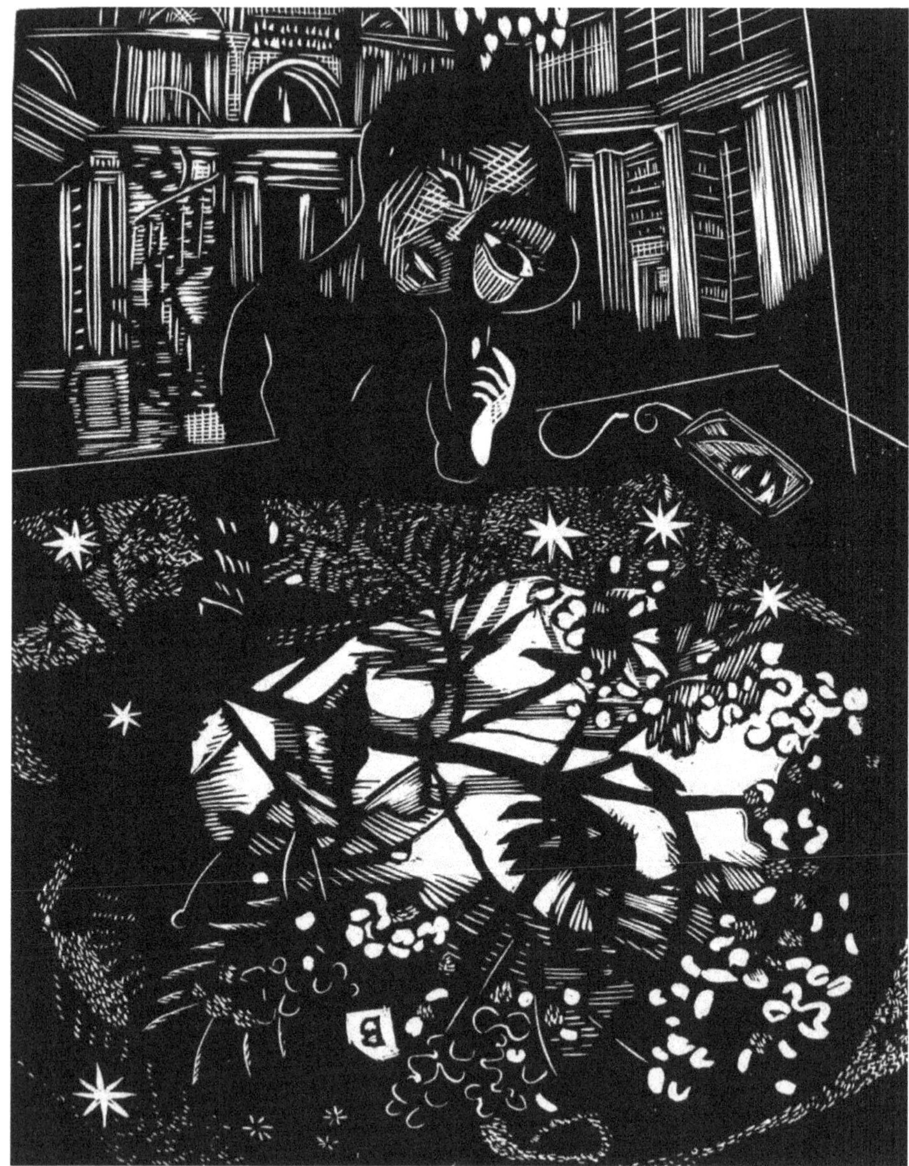

Dante – Seeking Immortality (2024) by Wuon-Gean Ho.
Linocut and Monoprint, 20 x 15 cm.

So fixed mine eyes were, in resolve entrenched
so deep, their ten years' thirst to satiate,
that all my other faculties were quenched;

and of this side and that of them were set
high walls of unconcern, the holy smile
so drew them to itself in the old net:

until those goddesses in forceful style
turned my gaze leftward, for: "Too fixedly!"
I heard one say, when I had looked awhile;

and that condition which we often see
in eyes but lately smitten by the sun,
for a short time thereafter blinded me.

Purgatorio 32.1–12

Dante - Seeking Immortality. This image is about the quest for knowledge that was performed in the Taylor Institute Library. The artist holds a magnifying glass to her eye, which shows more of the eye itself than what the eye might be witnessing. The print questions how much can be found by slow observation, and how much of the maker is revealed in this study. The flower depicted is an acacia, chosen because it signified immortality to ancient Greeks and ancient Hebrews. The girl hidden in the branches of the acacia is labelled with a capital B to signify Beatrice. She is surrounded by stars.

WGH

Virgil is not the only guide who leads Dante through the Afterlife. When they arrive at the top of the mountain of Purgatory, Virgil disappears and Dante comes face to face with the woman he loved on earth, Beatrice. Their reunion is not depicted in the way we might expect. After being scolded by her, Dante finds himself blinded by Beatrice's beauty. This experience continues as they journey into Paradise, but he does not take his eyes off her. Indeed, although it blinds him, looking at Beatrice becomes a way for Dante to see more. When the light of heaven becomes too much: he turns his eyes back to Beatrice.

RB

Overleaf: *Dante – Bodbib Press* (2024) by Wuon-Gean Ho.
Linocut and Monoprint, 15 x 20 cm.

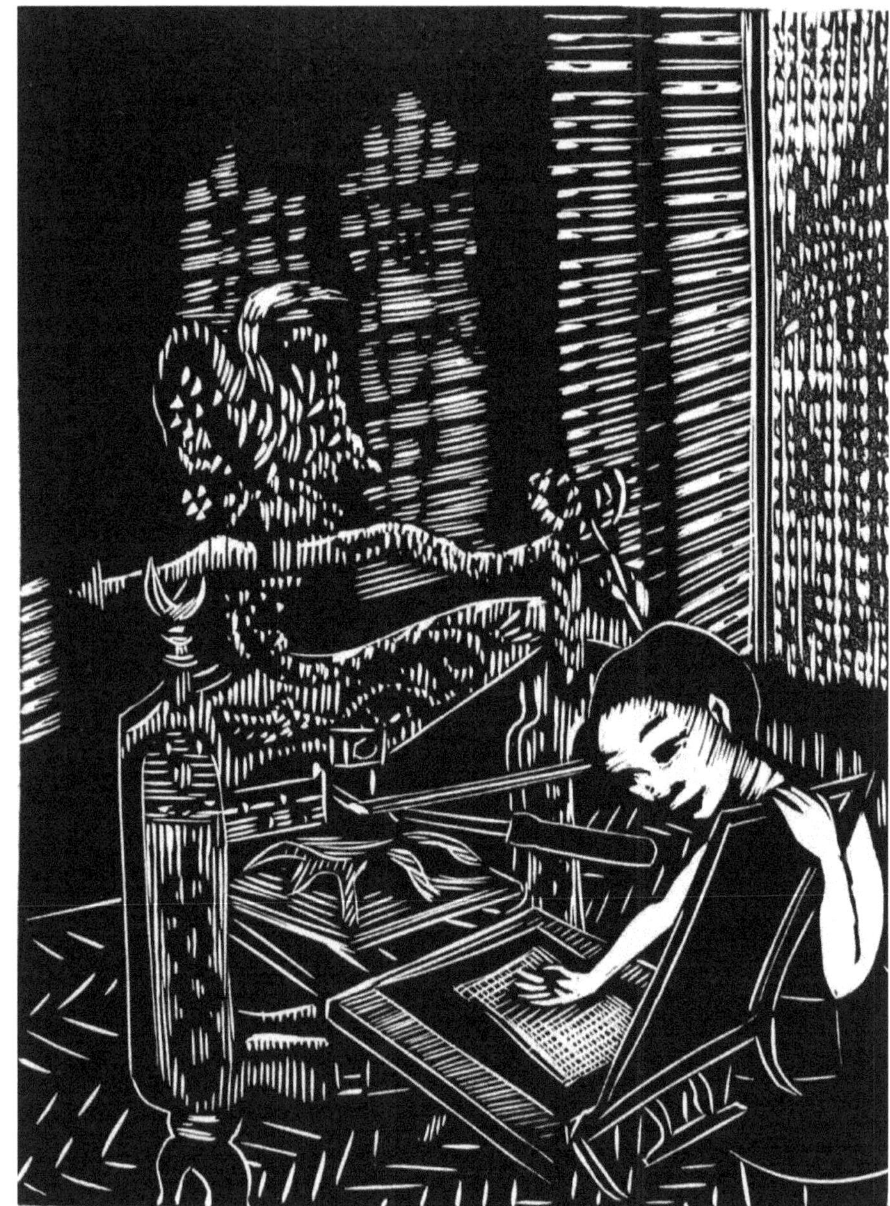

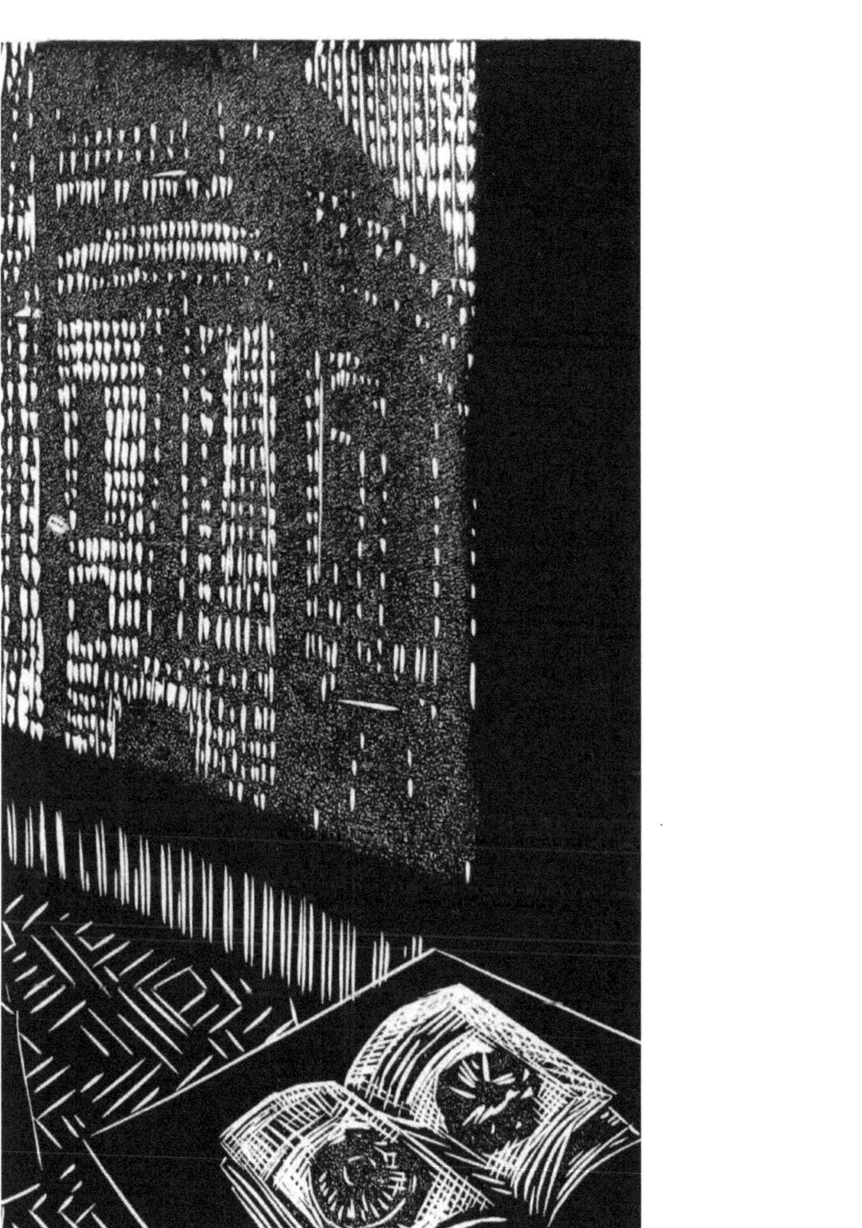

Remain now, Reader, still upon thy bench,
in thought pursuing that which is foretasted,
if thou wouldst jocund be instead of weary.

I've set before thee; henceforth feed thyself,
for to itself diverteth all my care
that theme whereof I have been made the scribe.

Paradise 10.7–15

Dante - Bodbib Press. This print is about the labour of creating a physical print with carved block, ink, paper and a cast-iron printing press. The studio depicted is the Bodleian Library Press in Oxford, which is a magnificent workshop. On sunny days the light shines through the tall stone windows and makes beautiful shadows on the walls. From the window, a shimmering vision of the Radcliffe camera can be seen. The book in the corner of the print has circular map-like images which reference the circular shapes of some of the images of hell in the edition printed by Marcolini in 1544.

WGH

Dante - Bodbib Press immerses us in the world of the printmaker, capturing a moment of reflection as the artist brings her images to life. Dante's poem is present in the open book that recalls the layout of a sixteenth-century edition of the *Divine Comedy* and, perhaps, on the sheet of paper that Wuon-Gean smooths on the press with the back of her hand. Transposed from a reader's bench to a printer's studio, this scene recalls the anticipation evoked by Dante when he pauses his narration in *Paradiso*, asking us, the readers, to reflect on what might happen before his poem continues.

RB

Overleaf: *Dante – Star* (2024) by Wuon-Gean Ho. Linocut, 15 x 20 cm.

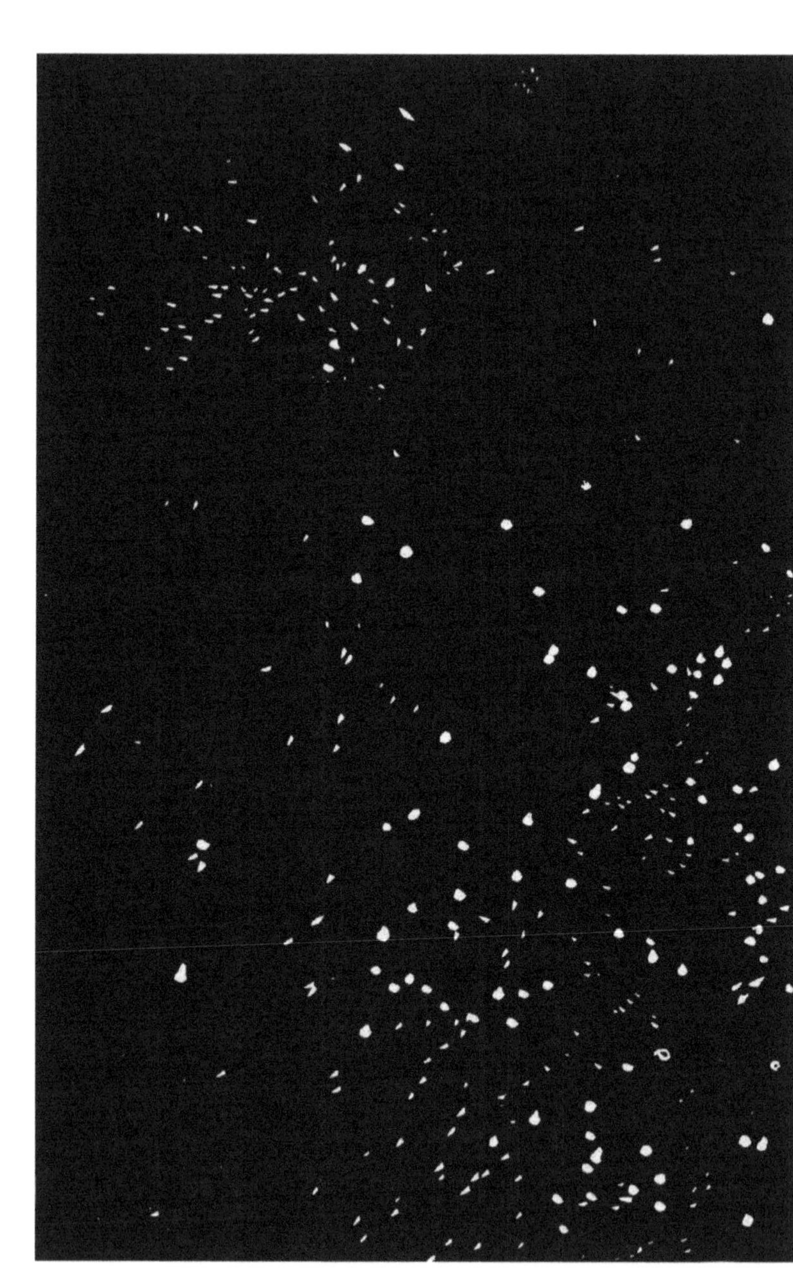

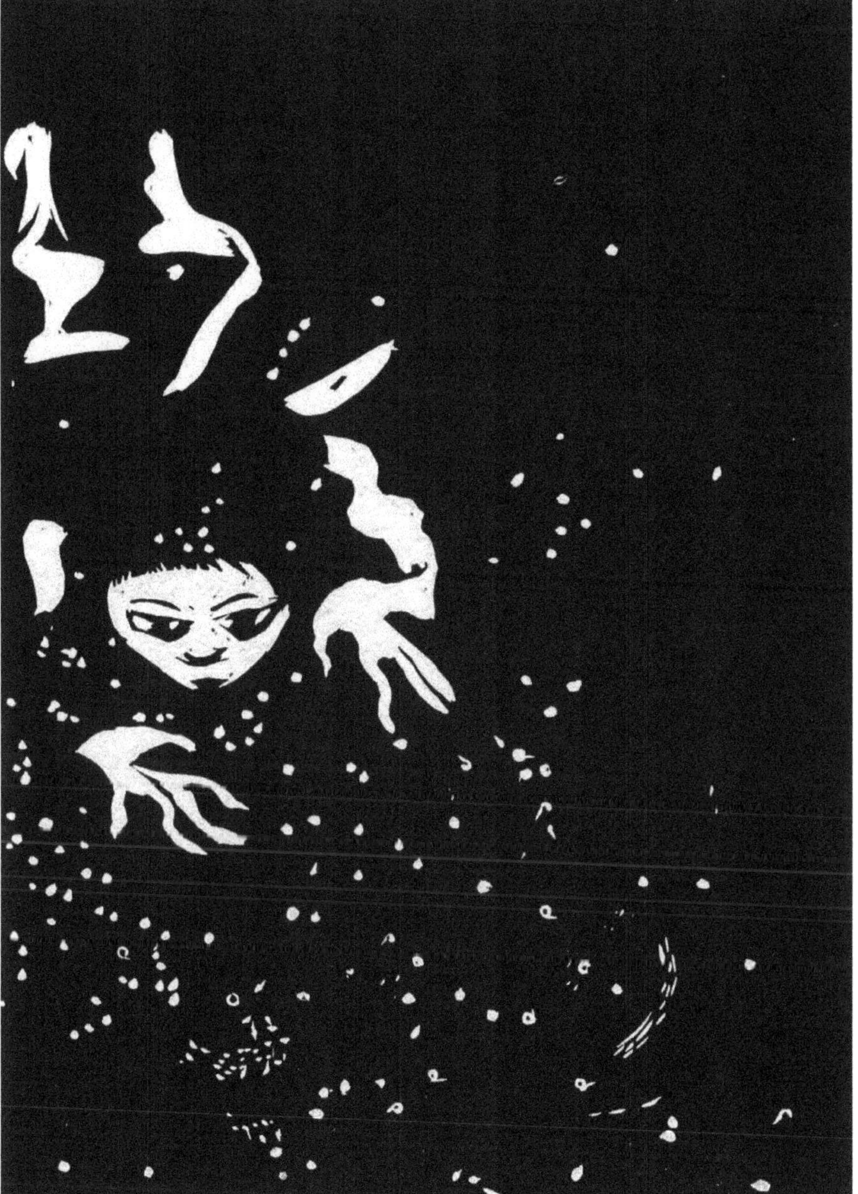

Sunward I fixed mine eyes beyond their wont.
(...)
Not long I bore it, nor so little awhile
but I beheld it sparkle round about
like iron that comes molten from the fire;

and suddenly it seemed that day to day
was added, as if He who has the power
had with another sun the heaven adorned.

(...) Inwardly I became
like Glaucus, tasting of the herb that made him
peer of the other gods beneath the sea.

Paradise 1.54; 58–63; 67–69

Dante - Star. When Dante emerges into the heavens he is surrounded by light. Here he is depicted swimming, like a frog, into a new dimension. He is surrounded with many more stars than in any of the illustrations. This is because the old images show stars as having a fixed number of points, floating in organised grids, whereas the ones in this print are shown as specks and dots of light.

WGH

As he enters Paradise, Dante describes a miraculous transformation. Comparing himself to a fisherman from classical mythology, Dante calls himself Glaucus, a man turned into a sea monster so that he could pursue a nymph with whom he had fallen in love. This maritime metamorphosis is recalled in the amphibian-like form chosen to present the paradisiacal state in *Dante - Star*. The molten metal that Dante describes as he looks into the sun becomes the spark-like stars that constellate this print and accompany Dante all the way to the end of poem, which closes in sight of 'the love that moves the sun and other stars' (*Paradiso* 33.145).

RB

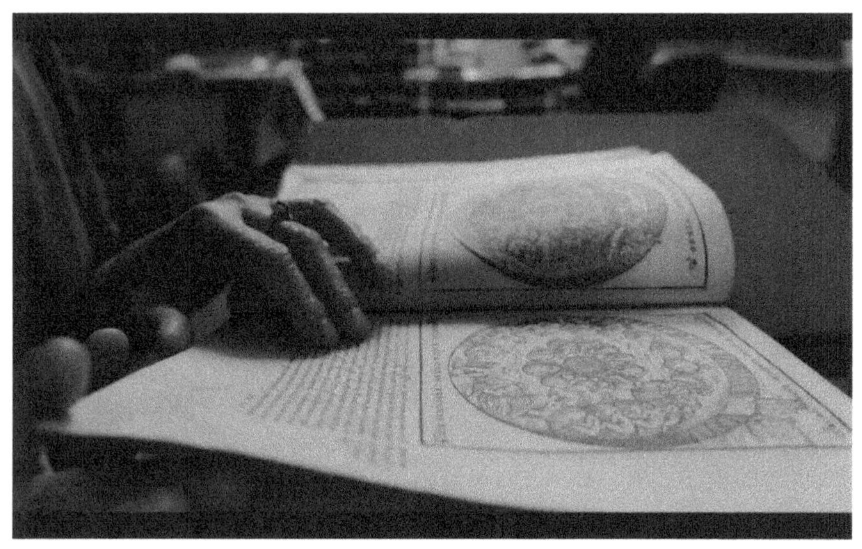

Still from *'Looking for Dante'* (2024). Film by Wuon-Gean Ho.

Music by Steve Baker. 3 minutes 43 seconds

Looking for Dante is a short film that reflects upon the artist's engagement with the project and her process of making the prints. It begins, "This is a tale within a tale within a tale. 700 years after the writing of the *Divine Comedy*, I sit, just after Easter, on a rainy Buffalo day, watching the grey sky and the ever-replenishing puddles. I am looking for the context."

The mention of Easter refers to the setting of the *Divine Comedy* over three days of Easter. The haptic, sensed, felt nature of engaging with early printed texts is shown with the careful handling of old paper and close examination of the ink and forms held within each page. The making of new images is shown with precise drawing and carving and the act of printing in the Bodleian press. The music was composed specifically for the piece by Steve Baker and conveys some of the curiosity and care that drove the research.

The video shows the strength of subjective positions, situated in the contemporary world. It contends that embodied physical practice might be used as a sharp tool to unpick questions about the past.

WGH

Scan the QR code to watch the film.

Looking for Dante: Part II

Reflections on Dante

Wuon-Gean Ho

This project, initiated by researchers Simon Gilson and Rebecca Bowen, began as a call for a contemporary artist to respond to early printed editions of Dante's *Divine Comedy* held in the collection of the Taylorian Institute at the University of Oxford. As an artist-printmaker, I make most of my work using relief printmaking, which is a similar technique to the images in the books of concern. However, I had only superficial knowledge of Dante and had not seen many printed books from this time.

We started the collaboration by viewing a selection of books in the beautiful Taylorian Library. The detailed scholarship of Simon and Rebecca was instantly clear. They spoke with warmth and clarity on general themes, then picked out a few storylines to entice me into Dante's world. These passages of text included the love affair of Paolo and Francesca; the specific topography of the layers of hell; Dante's guidance by Virgil and Beatrice; Dante's spiritual evolution; how Dante does not eat nor sleep but does faint, and so on. We spoke of forces behind the creation of this kind of luxury book: issues such as funding streams; the time investment of publishing houses and technical printers (in terms of paper, block carving and typesetting) in creating such an ambitious work; the spaces left on the page for crests and bespoke modifications that would have allowed wealthy patrons to state their ownership; and the assertion of scholarship in books with commentaries and notes in the margins.

Over the course of the following months I went back to the library to look at the books alone. I was thrilled to turn the crisp pages, to feel the embossed traces of ink on paper. I marvelled at the woodcuts and spent time using drawing as a way of translating the motives behind the creation of the iconography to gain a deeper understanding. The books became wordless but generous guides and teachers, and my responses, equally wordless, are located in the creation of new work.

However, as a contemporary artist, I was also informed by the nature of what it means to live in the present day. I sought to reframe the concepts from the books with current events. I wanted to make a comparison between our interaction with the portable networked screen (mobile phone technology and so on) with the impact achieved by the innovation of analogue print technology and subsequent dissemination of printed texts.

The project started the same week as violence erupted in Israel then in Gaza, against a backdrop of ongoing conflict in Ukraine and the rumble of climate emergency. Suddenly the concept of hell as a place to punish those who have done wrong became disingenuous. What did it mean to do wrong 700 years ago, compared to the depths of today? To which circle of hell would we allocate those who orchestrate the deprivation of entire communities of food and water; the use of dirty bombs; deforestation; unfair taxation? And what of those who set innocent trees alight?

Two books stood out and I returned to them again and again. The first is Taylorian shelfmark ARCH.FOL.IT.1491 (printed by Codecà in 1491) which attracted me for the graphic quality of the storytelling. I was sad not to find the name of the artist, let alone the carver, because the images are beautifully constructed: tight, full of drama, and surprising details, utilising the space and format on the page to full advantage. On the whole the protagonist is depicted moving through the scene using a flat depth of field, delineated with stylized taut lines, sometimes depicted more than once in each tableau, generally mimicking paintings from the medieval period prior to 1300s. In the corners: castles and hillsides. Beasts with wings tumble and writhe. Dante, in profile, sports a frog-like eye and a page-boy hairdo.

In the process of examining these images, I came to wonder whether they were a deliberate graphic throwback to the iconography of Dante's lifetime, rather than reflecting the state of art-making in

Renaissance Italy. After all, even Giotto, who painted in the early 1300s, had developed a greater sense of movement and perspective than is evident in the illustrations in this edition printed by Codecà in 1491, when by then a young Leonardo da Vinci had been painting soft volumetric figures for more than a dozen years.

The second is the book labelled Taylorian shelfmark ARCH.8o.IT.1544 (printed by Marcolini in 1544) to which I returned again and again because of the sudden contemporary burgeoning of the figure. Here are many virtuoso crowd scenes. The gluttonous lie in their pit, being rained on by a convincing cloud. The mass of sinners lament. The flat top of purgatory's mountain (supposedly the Garden of Eden) is bushy, the three-headed dog has a touch of trainable vigour. I was puzzled as to why the first set of illustrations in the book depicted fresh, bright images which appear to me, as a fellow artist, to have an honesty to their mark. Later on in the same volume similar compositions appear, but now reinterpreted, almost parodied. A softer, bigger, blacker cloud. A less convincing dog. Fatter but less corporeal gluttons. Were the first fresh blocks lost? Did they run out of funds to pay the original artist?

My observations and study of the printed books did not result in images that illustrate specific texts. However, the scope of Dante's writing covers many of the same forces and motives. It has been very pleasing to have Rebecca and Simon's suggestions for accompanying text from the *Divine Comedy* placed alongside each image.

As my process of making is directly informed by observation and lived experience, it felt appropriate to insert myself into the scene, in a similar way that Dante takes the reader on a journey with himself as the pilgrim. Like Dante, I also had knowledgeable guides: two of them human, two of them books. In other parallels, the project commenced when I was looking for a new print studio. I was fortunate to be invited to print in the workshop of the Bodleian Library Press, located in the heart of Oxford, and later, even further afield, in Mirabo press, Buffalo, New York. The prints and film were made as a result of this creative journey.

Printing the 'Divine Comedy'

Simon Gilson

Dante's great poetic masterpiece, the *Commedia* or *Comedy*, was one of the first vernacular texts to be printed with moveable type in Italy. The first edition was produced in the small town of Foligno in 1472, some 40 kilometres southeast of Perugia, and the poem was reprinted quite often during the fifteenth and sixteenth centuries. There were at least another fifteen editions (or incunables) in the early period of printing before 1501; a further twenty-three editions of the whole poem or parts of it are known to have been printed in Italy before 1600. Oxford and its many libraries contain a wealth of early print copies of Dante, holding hundreds of copies of his *Comedy* and other works that were printed in these centuries. The Taylor Institution Library alone holds at least twenty-six editions of the *Commedia* printed before 1596, the last print of the sixteenth century. This essay presents a panorama of what it meant to print Dante in the late fifteenth and sixteenth centuries. It aims to do this by considering four of the editions that were repeatedly called upon as part of the collaboration with the artist and print maker, Wuon-Gean Ho.

Our first edition, and the oldest printed copy of the *Commedia* held in the Taylorian collections, is an incunable printed in Venice by the German craftsman Windelin of Speyer (Vindelino da Spira in the Italian version of his name) who, though his printshop concentrated on printing classical and legal texts, had already printed the very first edition of Petrarch's vernacular poetry in 1470. Windelin's edition of Dante's *Commedia*, also printed in Venice, dates to 1477.

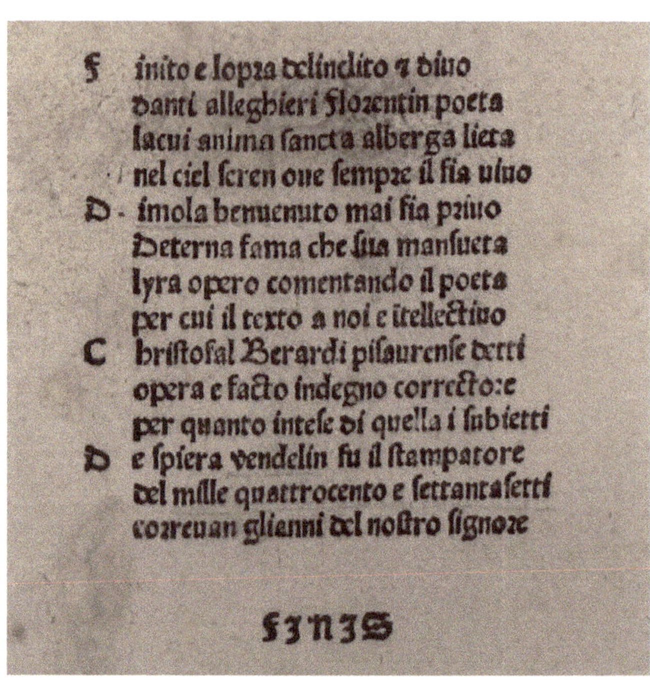

F inito e lopra delinclito e diuo
danti allegbieri Florentin poeta
lacui anima ſancta alberga lieta
nel ciel ſeren oue ſempre il ſia uiuo
D imola benuenuto mai ſia priuo
Deterna fama che ſua manſueta
lyra opero comentando il poeta
per cui il texto a noi e itellectiuo
C briſtofal Berardi piſaurenſe detti
opera e facto indegno corrector
per quanto inteſe di quella i ſubietti
D e ſpiera vendelin fu il ſtampatore
del mille quattrocento e ſettantaſetti
correuan glianni del noſtro ſignore

FINIS

Fig. 1. Colophon, Speyer, 1477, ARCH.FOL.IT.1477

A particularly astute publisher, Windelin was aware that previous editions of Dante's poem had provided relatively little supplement and assistance for readers. The large folio edition of Dante produced by his workshop aimed to fill this gap in the market by providing a printed text with commentary. The undertaking was technically and financially challenging. Windelin worked with a little-known figure, one Cristoforo Berardi of Pesaro, who took on the role of editor (*correttore* in Italian) and proof reader, a very important job in the busy confusion of the printshop where each letter had to be carefully set for the moveable type to correctly reproduce the text. We know of his role in part because the colophon (a device at the very end of the printed book that provides valuable information about the identity of the printer and other agents involved in its creation, including the place and date of the printing process) takes the form of a sonnet that notes the role of the 'unworthy corrector' and records his name (fig. 1). It was most probably Berardi who wrote this sonnet and who also prepared the text of Dante and of the commentary accompanying it, as well as other features of the edition, including the punctuation, the summaries of each canto and *cantica*, and even a life of the author.

The *mise-en-page* of the Windelin edition is stylishly balanced throughout the book, with two columns used for the text of Dante, the summaries and the life, and for the commentary, too. The margins are ample and an elegant gothic typeface is used: this is unusual as other prints of Dante are in the less-Germanic, Roman type, but also understandable given Windelin's production of academic legal texts, which were almost always printed in gothic. The life of Dante, written by Giovanni Boccaccio in the 1350s, is printed on the first pages of Windelin's edition and is the first ever printing of Boccaccio's celebrated biography. It is followed by summaries (or rubrics) of each *cantica* and then by a series of summaries for each canto of the *Inferno* (similar content is provided for the other two *cantiche*, *Purgatorio* and *Paradiso*, before each part of the poem). Spaces are left for the inclusion of hand-coloured or even illuminated initials to be added at the beginning of each canto, with an even larger space left at the beginning of each canticle; these elements would be added later in a separate phase of the life of the book (fig. 7). Many of the 120 copies of Windelin's edition that survive to this day display such hand decorations. The commentary is in the Italian vernacular, a text that is even older than Boccaccio's life of Dante: it was composed by the Bolognese scholar Iacomo della Lana in the late 1320s and was the first full commentary to the entire poem, one that circulated very extensively in manuscripts. Lana's commentary, though outdated by the time Windelin made his edition over 150 years later in 1477, is rich in scientific, philosophical and theological explanations, and this helps to confer a strong academic imprint on the overall presentation of Dante's poem.

After the edition and commentary, there are two poems that give an overview of the *Commedia* (both its topography and its allegorical features). These are also often found in the extensive manuscript tradition and include the *capitoli* by one of Dante's sons, Jacopo Alighieri, and by an early cultivator of Dante, Bosone da Gubbio. The volume concludes with some pseudonymous verses, the so-called 'Credo di Dante', often attributed to Dante himself but actually penned by another author and telling of Dante's supposed conversion from love poet to pious Christian author. Presented as a poem worthy of commentary and the kind of introductory paratext that we might expect in one of Windelin's editions of classical or legal texts, this edition of Dante confers an academic weight to the *Comedy*, one suggested too by its large folio format and gothic font, encouraging readers to see the poem as one of the literary greats.

The second oldest edition of Dante's *Commedia* in the Taylorian collections is also a large folio copy in which the role of the *correttore* is important. This edition contains Dante's verses, a commentary upon them, and a range of other features to assist the reader, including printed illustrations. Indeed this is the first fully illustrated Dante in print, as Rebecca Bowen notes in her contribution to this catalogue. The edition comes from the Venetian printshop of Bernardino Benali and Matteo Capcasa di Parma, better known as Codecà, and is dated 3 March 1491 (the date is important as this edition was followed by a similar but not identical edition on 18 November of the same year). Codecà, or Matteo of Parma as he was also known, was active in Venice as a printer of books under his own name and under those of others. He engaged in collaborations, like the one with Bernardino Benali that led to this edition of Dante, and produced a range of books in both Latin and vernacular Italian across a variety of genres.

Matteo's March edition of the *Commedia* has an extended colophon which, like the sonnet-colophon in Windelin's edition, provides us with valuable information about the agents involved in the book's production. Dante's work, in this colophon, is said to be 'illustrious and divine' ('inclito & divo') and we learn that the key figure, the *correttore*, was one 'reverend master Pietro da Figino, teacher of theology and excellent preacher of the order of the minors'. Pietro was a Tuscan theologian whom we know was indeed active as a preacher in Venice in the late 1480s and whose story offers a revealing example of how the Venetian presses made good use of migrant Tuscans in editing printed vernacular texts at a time in which the Italian language was not codified and people spoke dialects that varied completely from region to region.

The colophon also notes how the text was corrected and moved around to make up for the negligence of earlier printers – one senses the degree of competition and rivalry here between the many Venetian print shops. Finally, the colophon notes that the edition has put in the margins all the notable stories and the proper names that are found in the work ('& ha a[n]chora posto di fora i[n] li margini tutte le historie nota[n]de & li nomi p[ro]prii che si trovano i[n] ditta opera'). These printed marginalia, which run throughout the edition, deal with major historical and mythological figures as well as interpretations of the text, and are an important feature, helping to guide the reader not through Dante's text, but rather through the accompanying commentary by the Florentine scholar Cristoforo Landino, first printed a decade earlier (in 1481) and one of the most successful and widely reprinted commentaries on Dante in the Renaissance.

The *mise-en-page* of the edition as a whole is notable as it contains elegant woodcut initials and elaborately carved illustrations at the start of each canto, with full-page decorations at the start of each *cantica* (fig. 2). It also divides Dante's text up into blocs of verse with Landino's commentary surrounding them (and almost always taking up much more space on the page than the single column presentation of the poem). Once more the edition closes with a trilogy of pseudo-Dantean *terza rima* poems, the 'Credo di Dante', 'Pater nostro', and 'Ave maria'.

Unlike Windelin's edition of five years earlier, Codecà's edition engages with the visual potential of Dante's poem as much as its academic status. Alongside the extensive commentary that at times dwarfs or even engulfs the poem in terms of space on the page and focuses on the intellectual and literary endeavour of the poet, the woodcut illustrations placed at the start of every canto engage the reader in the pilgrim's journey that is the heart of the text.

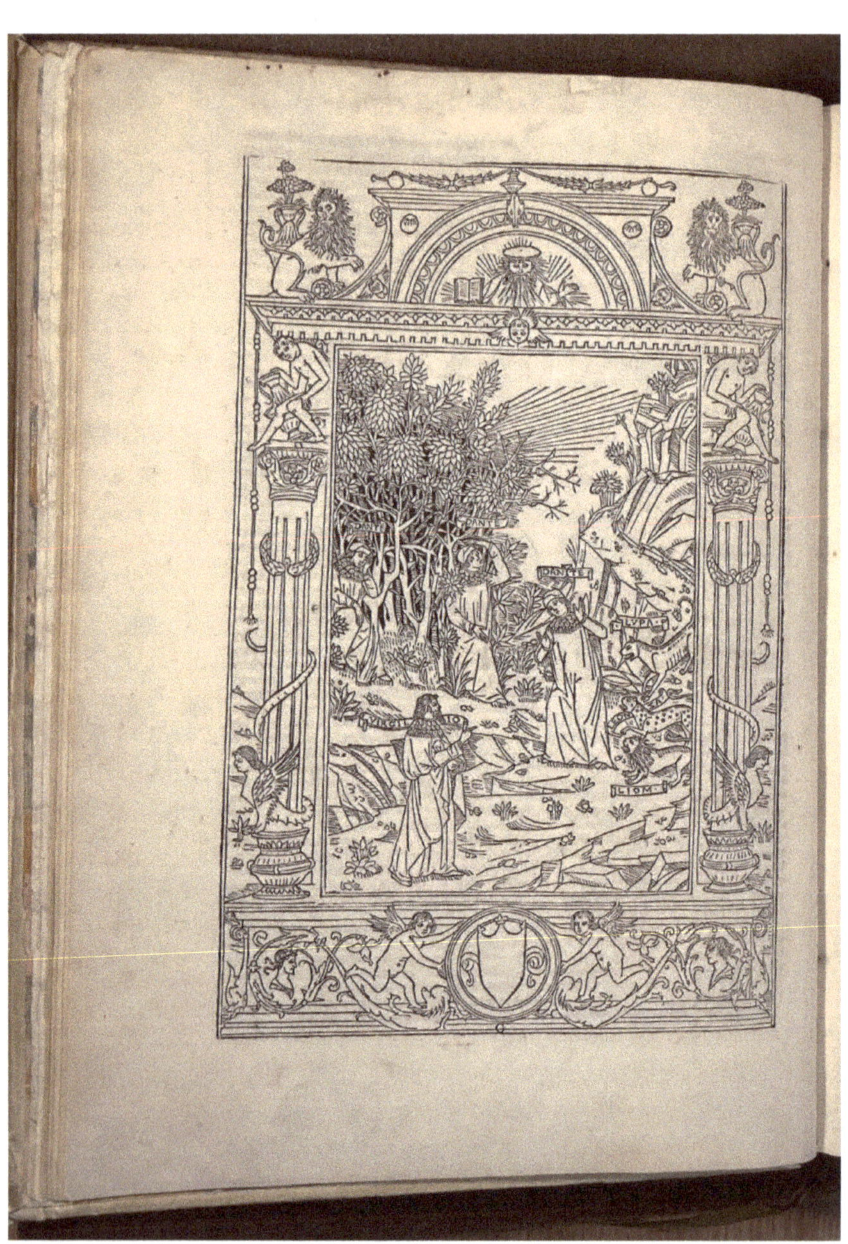

DANTE
DANTE
LVPA
LIOM

CANTO PRIMO DELLA PRIMA CANTICA OVERO COMEDIA DEL DIVINO POETA FIORENTINO DANTHE ALEGHIERI: CAPITOLO PRIMO.

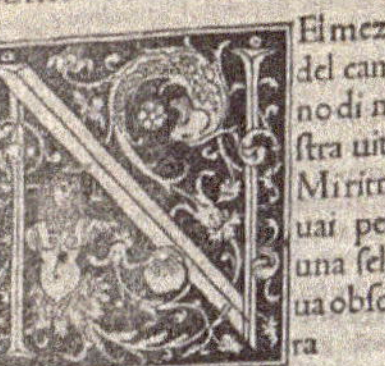

El mezo del camino di nostra uita
Mi ritrouai per una selua obſcura
che la diritta uia era ſmarrita
He quanto a dir quale era e coſa dura
eſta ſelua ſeluaggia & aſpra & forte
che nel penſier rinuoua la paura
Tanto e amara che poco e piu morte
ma per tractar del bẽ chio ui trouai
diro dellaltre coſe chio uho ſcorte
I non ſo ben ridir chomio uentrai
tãtera pien di ſonno i ſu quel pũcto
che la uerace uia abbandonai
Ma poi chio fui appie dũ colle giũto
la oue terminaua quella ualle
che mauea di paura el cor cõpõcto.
Guardai in alto & uidi le ſue ſpalle
ueſtite gia deraggi del pianeta
che mena dricto altrui p ogni calle:
Allhor fu la paura un pocho queta
che nellago del cuor mera durata
la nocte chio paſſai con tanta pieta

Habbiamo narrato nõ ſolamente la uita del poeta & el titolo del libro & che choſa ſia poeta Ma etiã quanto ſia uetuſta & anticha quanto nobile & uaria quãto utile & iocon da tal doctrina. Quanto ſia efficace a muouere lhumane menti: & quãto dilecti ogni liberale ingegno. Ne giudicammo da tacere quanto in ſi diuina diſciplina ſia ſta ta la excellentia dello ingegno del noſtro poeta. Inche ſi ſono ſtato piu brieue che forſe non ſi conuerebbe: conſideri che legge che la numeroſa & quaſi infinita coppia delle choſe delle quali e neceſſario tractare miſforza nõ uolendo chel uolume creſca ſopra modo: a inculcare & inuiluppare piu toſto che explicare & diſtẽdere molte choſe: & maxime quelle lequali quãdo ben taceſſi nõ pero ne reſtera obſcura la expoſitiõe del texto. Verremo adunq a quella. Ma perche ſtimo non eſſer lectore alcuno ne di ſi baſſo ingegno: ne di ſi pocho giudicio: che hauendo inteſo: quanto ſia & la profondita & uarieta della doctrina: & la excellẽtia & diuinita dello ingegno del noſtro toſcano: & fiorentino poeta: nõ ſi perſuada che queſto principio del primo canto debba per ſublimita & grãdezza eſſer pari alla ſtupenda doctrina delle choſe che ſeguitano: pero chon ogni induſtria inueſtighere mo che allegoricho ſenſo arechi ſeco queſto mezo del camino: & che choſa ſia ſelua. Diche ueggio nõ piccola differentia eſſere ſtata tra glinterpreti & expoſitori di queſta cantica. Impero che alchuni dicono: che il mezo della uita humana e el ſonno moſſi: credo dalla ſentẽtia daryſtotile dicẽdo lui nelletica neſſunna differentia eſſere tra felici: & miſeri nella meta dela uita: perche le nocti che ſono la meta del tempo cinducono ſonno: & da quello naſce che ne bene ne male ſentir poſſiamo. Il perche uogliono queſti: che el poeta pongha el mezo della uita per la nocte: & la nocte pel ſõno: ad notare che queſto poema non ſia altro che una uiſione che gli apparue dormẽdo per la quale hebbe cognitione delle choſe dal lui deſcripte in queſte tre comedie. Dicono adunq che lui imita Ioãni euãgeliſta el quale dormẽdo ſopra el pecto di chriſto redẽptore hebbe uiſione delle choſe celeſte: oueramẽte ponghi la nocte dimoſtrãdo lui hauere cominciato el ſuo poema di nocte nella quale racogliẽdoſi lanimo i ſe medeſimo & abſoluendoſi & liberãdoſi da ogni cura meglo intenda. Ma ben che tale ſentẽtia quadri al poeta: niẽtedimeno le parole nõ la dimoſtrono ſenon chon tãta obſcura ambiguita: che nõ pare degna della elegãtia di tanto poeta. Prima perche nõ ſeguita che bẽche nelle reuolutioni del tẽpo tãto ſpatio occupin le nocti quanto e di: per queſto dicẽdo io ſcripſi di nocte ſintenda io ſcripſi nel mezo della uita eta: pche & nel pricipio & nel fine della eta humana ſõno le nocti chome nel mezo & ſimelmẽte e di. Il perche p la medeſima ragione ſi poti ebbe fare tale interpretatione pel di chome per la nocte. Altri dicono che uolle pel mezo del camino itendere che nel mezo delleta dette pricipio al ſuo poema. Ma nõ e una medeſima opinione del termine dela noſtra eta: pche diuerſi ſcriptori diuerſamẽte ſentono. Ariſtotile nel ſuo de republica pare che approui la ſentẽtia di certi poeti: iquali diuiſono la eta p numero ſeptenario attribuẽdo. E primi ſepte alla infantia: E ſecondi alla pueritia: E terti che peruẽgono auctuno ala adoleſcentia. Dipoi pongono due ſeptenarii per la giouẽtu & arriuono a trẽtacinq: & qſta eta uole nel medeſimo luogho Ariſtotile che ſia perfecta a celebrare e matrimonio. Dopo la giouẽtu ſeguita la eta uirile la quale p due ſeptenarii arriua allãno nono & quadrageſimo: nel qual tẽpo per che glhuomini ſõno di pfecto cõſiglio: ne anchora hãno diminuite le forze del corpo giudica tãto philoſopho chel lhuomo ſia molto apto al gouerno della rep. Et finalmẽte pone el reſto delleta in tre ſeptenarii. Et uuole che el termine ſia ãni ſeptanta quaſi preſago della ſua morte: laquale fu nellãno ſeptuageſimo della ſua uita. Et maxime ſi moſſe a queſto: pche el numero ſeptenario ſi fa nõ ſolamẽte di ſepte: Ma ãchora ſi multiplica p dieci numero pfecto. Queſta medeſima ſententia e del pſalmiſta dicẽte: An-

Fig. 2. *Inferno* 1, Codecà, 1491, ARCH.FOL.IT.1491(1), (f. a1v & a2r)

As we move into the sixteenth century some significant innovations are made in the printing of Dante, although the legacy of Landino's commentary endures, as the editions in the Taylorian collections stand to prove. Another constant is the city of Venice as the most important place in Italy for the printing, circulation, and consumption of vernacular literature from the late fifteenth century onwards, though the Taylor also holds several editions that testify to interest in the poem from elsewhere, including ongoing Florentine engagements that provide patriotic reactions to Venetian appropriations. A major new innovation in the production of the printed Dante came with the printing of an elegant small-format edition of the *Commedia* in italic type by the press of the great Venetian typographer Aldus Manutius in 1502. This remarkably elegant typographical format was achieved with very careful editing and punctuation (the text was prepared by the Venetian courtier and humanist Pietro Bembo). Significantly, too, there is no commentary nor any illustrative cycles and a new title is used: *Le terze rime di Dante*, which does not stress Dante's Florentiness or divinity but the form of his poem. There is no copy of this edition in the Taylorian collections, but the library does hold a reprint of the edition released by Aldus and his father-in-law Andrea Torresano in 1515. This edition makes several editorial changes and introduces new paratexts, probably in response to other editions on the market.

In 1506 the Florentine Giunta press had published an edition prepared by the poet and scholar Girolamo Benivieni which included a dialogue on measurements in Hell, an interest also found in Landino's commentary. Aldus' 1515 edition seems to respond to this interest, bearing a new title ('Dante col sito, et forma dell'Inferno tratta dalla istessa descrittione del Poeta'), which gestures to this lively vein of discussion. The edition also presents three new woodcuts: a two-page map of Hell (fig. 14), and two interesting representations of the moral ordering of Hell and Purgatory, both in the form of schemes (fig. 3). One further addition is a dedicatory letter by Torresano to the young poetess, Vittoria Colonna, celebrating Dante's divinity, his status as a modern classic and his polymathic versatility.

Amongst the sixteenth-century editions presented here and viewed by Wuon-Gean Ho, after the large and prestigious study folios that we have discussed, we signal first a small format edition in octavo and not printed in Venice but nearby at Toscolano, a city on the shores of Lake Garda in Lombardy which, from 1300, was one of the most important sites for the production of paper in Italy. This edition was printed by Alessandro Paganini around 1520. Paganini had produced an earlier and more innovative edition in Venice some years before and in an even smaller format. The edition in the Taylor is the later one and, like Aldus' 1515 *Commedia*, it reproduces the poem with the title *Dante col sito et forma dell'Inferno*, reflecting a real vogue that had developed first in Florence by the 1430s.

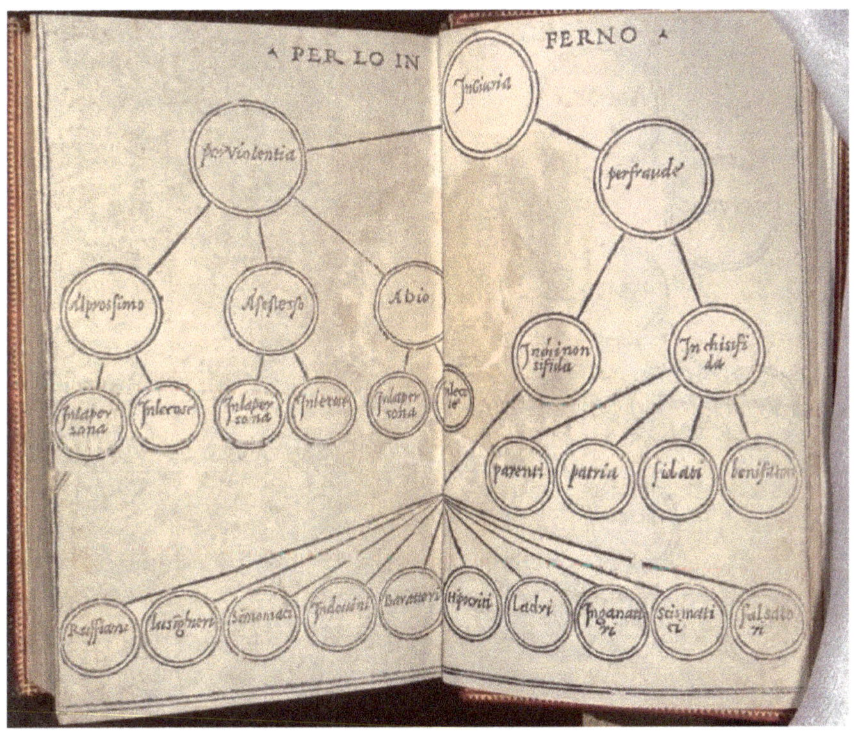

Fig. 3. Diagram of sins in *Inferno*, Aldus & Torresano, 1515, ARCH.8o.IT.1515(1), (ff. H6r& H6v)

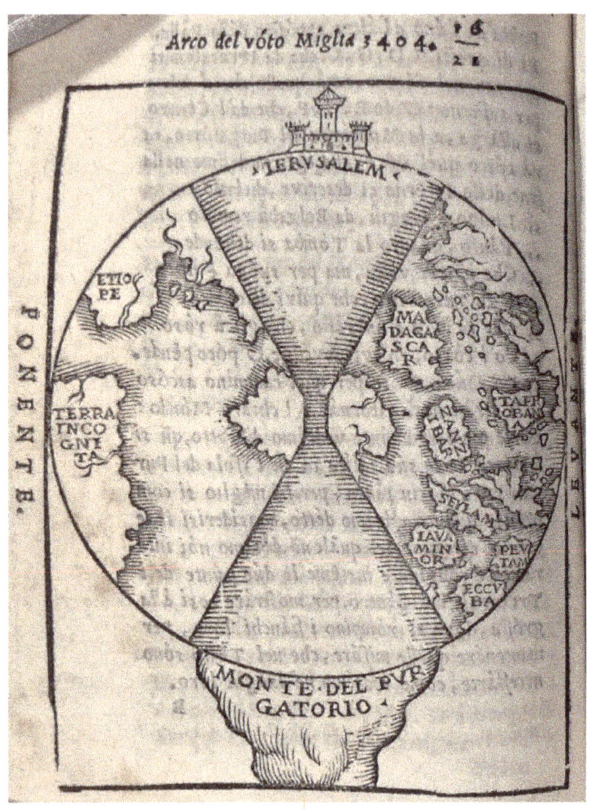

Interested in understanding, expounding, and drawing the measures, distances, and timeframes involved in the journey through the afterlife described in the *Comedy*, scholars began writing mathematical, cartographic treatises on Dante's fictional text. The commentary by Landino also built upon and contributed to these discussions; it includes a section in the prologue devoted to these topics, where Landino relays the views of Antonio Manetti, an earlier writer who had published on the shape of the *Inferno*. Later Florentine writers returned to the debate, which came to take on patriotic dimensions. Girolamo Benivieni, editor of the edition printed by Filippo Giunta in Florence in 1506, includes an entire dialogue with Manetti as an imagined interlocutor on the topic.

Above: Fig. 4. Location of Hell, Neri Dortelata, 1544, MOORE 4.A.29, (p. 18)

In the sixteenth-century, then, there developed a rich stream of discussions on the topography of Dante's afterlife and Dante's journey as protagonist through its realms. One remarkable document testifying to the ferment regarding the location, form and measurements of the afterlife, and especially of Hell, is a printed work by a Florentine academician, Pierfrancesco Giambullari under the pseudonym Neri Dortelata in 1544. Giambullari was a key figure in setting up the Florentine Academy, a Florentine state-sponsored institution for the promotion of vernacular learning; and he is the author of a commentary on the *Comedy* (now largely lost) and other linguistic treatises. Giambullari's treatise, *De'l sito*, puts into practice, with a new system of diacritical marks, part of a reformed orthography of the Italian language and discusses at length the topics covered in Manetti and Landino's earlier works. It also adds a variety of new insights and information, printing new maps, diagrams, and even tables for the various subdivisions and 'measures' of Hell, some of which follow the designs present in the edition printed by Giunta in Florence in 1506 and some of which present a new and more clearly scientific visual language (fig. 4).

This interest is also manifested in our next edition of Dante's poem, which is remarkable at multiple levels and elicited particular attention from Wuon-Gean. It is an edition and commentary, with extensive illustration and paratexts by a scholar from Lucca, Alessandro Vellutello (1473-1549?) who came to Venice in the mid-1520s. His Dante, a refined textual and graphical print, came out in 1544 from the print shop of Francesco Marcolini of Forlì, an artist and architect who was friends with Titian and a printer of books renowned for their typographical and illustrative refinement, with elegant *mise-en-page* and a richness and variety of woodcut illustrations. Before Dante's poem there are four main paratexts: a dedicatory letter to Pope Paul III (stressing Dante's religious orthodoxy in a period where this had begun to be questioned); an address to readers (dealing with issues of textual editing, the need for a new commentary, and his own interpretative method); a life of Dante; and a lengthy cosmographical account of Hell, the 'Descrizzione de lo Inferno', with diagrams.

de le uenti particolari parti, ne lequali habbiamo ueduto quello esser distinsto, faremo fine, e passeremo, (che ne pare hoggimai tempo) a piu necessaria, &

cosa.

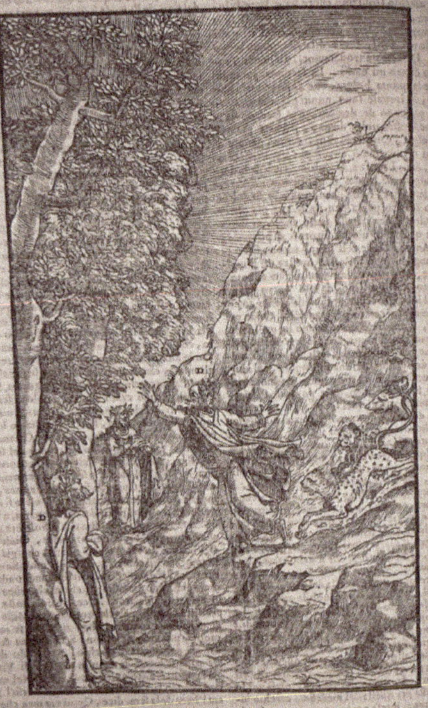

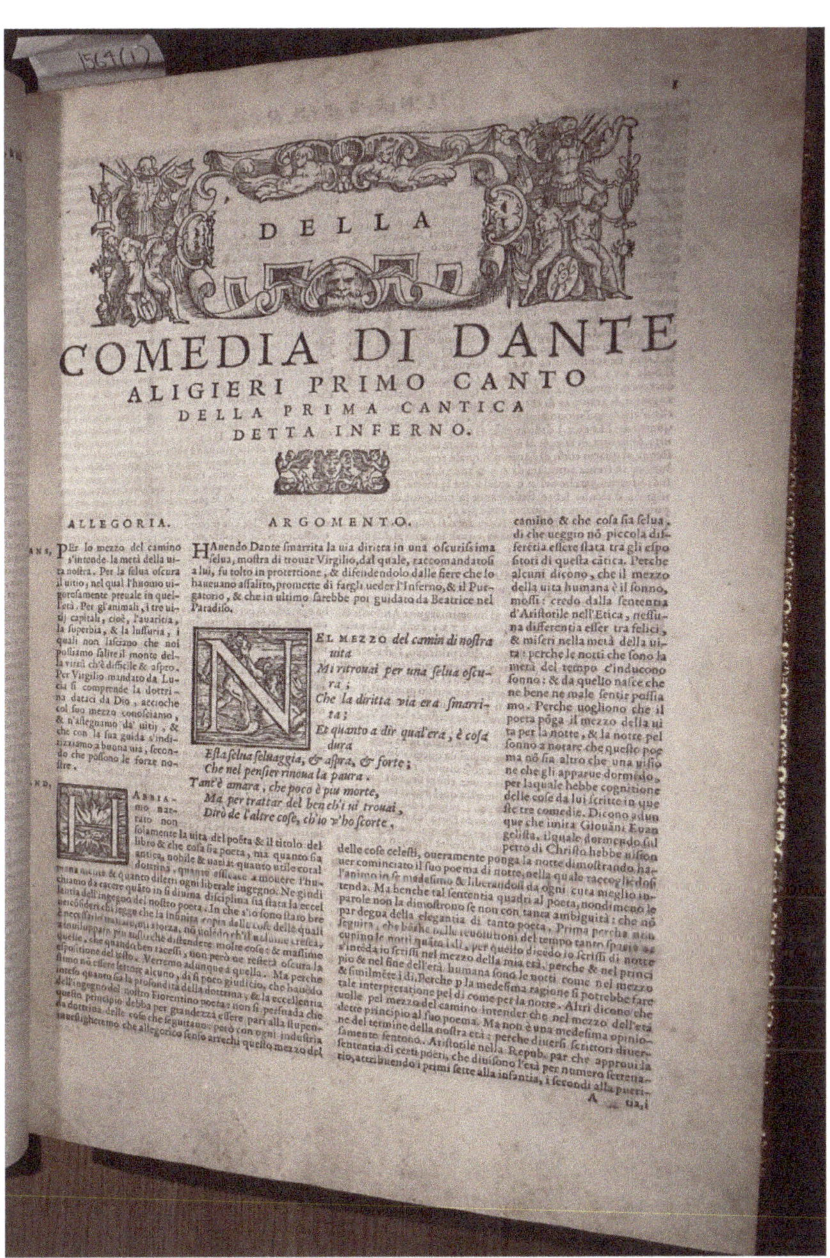

DELLA

COMEDIA DI DANTE ALIGIERI PRIMO CANTO DELLA PRIMA CANTICA DETTA INFERNO.

ALLEGORIA.

ARGOMENTO.

HAuendo Dante smarrita la uia diritta in una oscurissima selua, mostra di trouar Virgilio, dal quale, raccomandatosi a lui, fu tolto in protettione, & difendendolo dalle fiere che lo haueuano assalito, promette di fargli ueder l'Inferno, & il Purgatorio, & che in ultimo sarebbe poi guidato da Beatrice nel Paradiso.

NEl mezzo del camin di nostra uita
Mi ritrouai per una selua oscura;
Che la diritta via era smarrita;
Et quanto a dir qual'era, è cosa dura
Esta selua seluaggia, & aspra, & forte;
Che nel pensier rinoua la paura.
Tant'è amara, che poco è piu morte,
Ma per trattar del ben ch'i ui trouai,
Dirò de l'altre cose, ch'io v'ho scorte,

Fig. 5. *Inferno* 1, Sessa, 1564, ARCH.FOL.IT.1564 (1), (f. C1v)

Vellutello unleashes a number of polemics in these paratexts, against the Aldine editions (judged to have ruined the text of Dante with an open condemnation of Bembo's editorial work), against Landino (for slavish and plodding reliance on Benvenuto da Imola's earlier Latin commentary and on Boccaccio's 'Life of Dante'), and against the whole tradition of Florentine cosmographical enquiry into the site and dimensions of Hell, including Landino, Manetti, and Benvieni who are all named and criticized. The next essay comments more fully on the woodcuts and illustrative programme, but I would note here the original ways in which the commentary and images clarify and reinforce one another in this edition.

The *mise-en-page* is familiar from the early print tradition and what we have discussed so far: Vellutello's edition of the poem is presented in groups of *terzine* in a left-hand column which is surrounded by his own exposition or commentary. That exposition displays a prominent interest in literal textual commentary and in readability. Dante's text – with the other works of the author himself (especially the *Convivio*) – is paraphrased, reordered, and explained in line with the interpretative method set out in the address to readers. Earlier commentators, especially Landino, are repeatedly mined for information, in spite of the polemics set out against them in the opening section. Other sources are also exploited in new ways, including the Florentine chronicler, and near contemporary of Dante, Giovanni Villani. Stylistic and linguistic discussion is not absent but it is not a primary concern and nor is it as refined as the discussion in some other sixteenth-century writers on Dante. Vellutello's new commentary was both praised and criticized by later writers; and, for all his polemic against Landino, he did not succeed in entirely displacing the earlier Florentine commentator's work. In fact, Landino's commentary was reprinted three times in the second half of the sixteenth century and each time in a dual commentary edition that brought it together with Vellutello's exegesis on the same page. The first of these editions in the Taylor is the 1564 Venetian edition, printed by the Sessa shop – the heirs of Melchiorre or Marchio Sessa who were responsible for an earlier print of Dante's *Convivio* in 1531.

Identifiable by their delightful cat and mouse printer's emblem (fig. 6), the Sessa had a print shop in San Pier Maggiore Popolo on Via Nova in Venice. This edition returns to the monumental folio format, and is of similar dimensions to the March edition of 1491 (fig. 5). However, because of the dual commentary format adopted, the volume is much longer. The title page is revealing since it mentions both commentators and the efforts of the *correttore* – Francesco Sansovino – who has added indexes, short summaries and allegorical interpretations to the text, as well as reformatting it typographically and re-editing it textually. The title page offers other innovations, in particular its use of a new profile portrait of Dante in a large medallion portrait placed within a floriated oval frame surrounded by mythological figures and floreal elements (fig. 7). Often called the 'gran naso', or 'big nose' edition, this portrait is reminiscent of the iconographical features in earlier portraits of Dante by Giorgio Vasari and Agnello Bronzino.

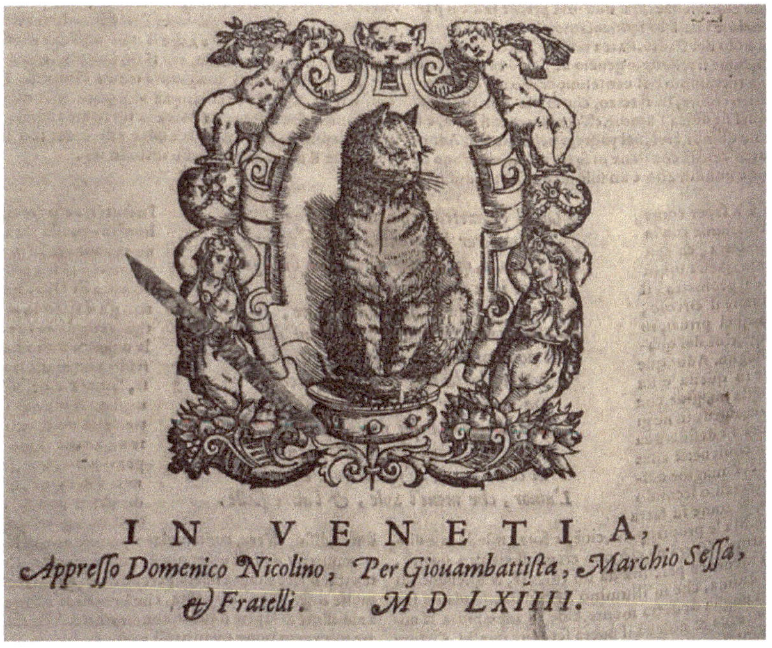

Fig. 6. Printer's device, Sessa, 1564, ARCH.FOL.IT.1564 (1)

Another Pope is implicated in this edition: this time in the dedication by Sansovino to Pope Pius IV. Dante is again presented as a model of piety and doctrinal orthodoxy. More paratexts follow this opening dedication, with a table of difficult words explaining and glossing Dante's language and even criticizing its impropriety at times – the sixteenth century is a period in which Dante's language was often considered to be linguistically rough and to involve poetically inappropriate themes. Typographically, the reprinting is notable for the way it marks up for the reader the text of Dante and his commentators, often through ornamental headpieces and print capitals.

The *mise-en-page* of the edition has two columns with the commentaries of Landino and Vellutello being indicated to readers in the margins by the letters LAND. and VELL (fig. 5). Dante's text is placed in the centre of the page. At the beginning of each canto there is an *argomento*, that is, a short narrative summary, which is also placed centrally. An *allegoria* (allegorical interpretation), usually attributed to Sansovino by means of the lettering SANV., is placed in the left-hand column. Dual commentaries had long been a feature in prints of Petrarch, and, beginning in the late fifteenth century, also in print editions of classical authors. Sansovino's edition shows how print was capable of repurposing Dante for readers interested in full-scale commentaries.

Our discussion has only touched on some of the prints of Dante produced in the fifteenth and sixteenth centuries and held in the Taylor Institution Library but it has allowed us to illustrate some of the many facets – commercial, technological, editorial, literary, linguistic, intellectual and philosophical – that influenced the presentation of the *Comedy* in print, as well as the accompanying strategies of printers and others involved in bringing the poem to readers in this period.

Facing page: Fig. 7. Title Page, Sessa, 1564, ARCH.FOL.IT.1564, (1)

DANTE

CON L'ESPOSITIONE DI CHRISTOFORO LANDINO, ET DI ALESSANDRO VELLVTELLO,

Sopra la sua Comedia dell'Inferno, del Purgatorio, & del Paradiso.

Con tauole, argomenti, & allegorie, & riformato, riueduto, & ridotto alla sua uera lettura,

PER FRANCESCO SANSOVINO FIORENTINO.

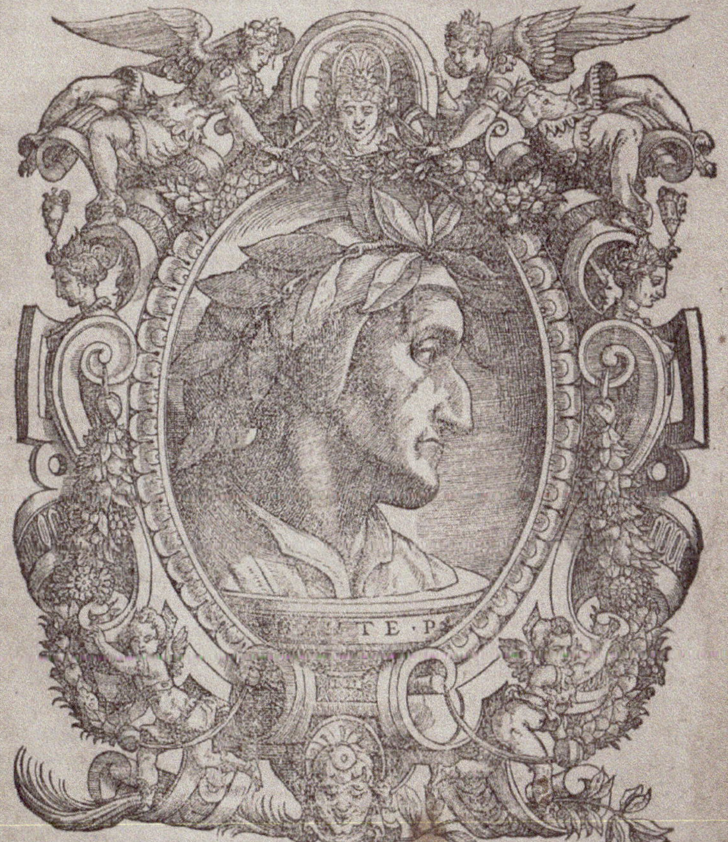

In Venetia, Appresso Giouambattista, Marchiò Sessa, & fratelli. 1564.

Seeing the 'Divine Comedy' in Early Print

Rebecca Bowen

The history of illustrating Dante in print begins before the first edition to include woodcuts or engravings. It begins in a blank space. In the 1470s, print technology was still new to Italy and very experimental. As part of the transition from manual to mechanised production, many of the centuries-old practices of making books by hand were retained and integrated with the new machine-assisted methods of printing. Spaces were left for artisanal interventions both in the supply chain and on the printed page: after the print shop, books would pass through the hands of multiple artisans to be bound and sometimes illuminated. The oldest print edition of Dante's *Comedy* housed in the Taylor Institution Library provides a case in point.

Printed by the German craftsman Windelin von Speyer in Venice in 1477, this large folio format book has an impressive presence but, to modern eyes, seems to have something missing. At the start of the poem, big blanks signal the space where the opening initials should appear. These blanks hold space for (and perhaps even encourage) the later inclusion of hand-painted decorations. Not all copies were treated to this service, like the copy in the Taylorian, where the blank spaces at the start of the different sections make painted initials seem like a ghostly possibility, present only in the mind of the reader who must imagine the missing letter in order to read the text (fig. 8).

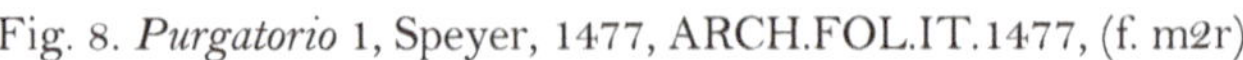

Purgatorio

Comincia la seconda parte della commedia di Dante allegbieri di firenze. Nel laquale parte si purgano li cõmessi peccati ⁊ vitii de quali luomo e confesso ⁊ pentuto cõ animo di satisfactione ⁊ cõtiene. xxxiii. Cãti. Qui el primo Canto sono quelli che sperano di venire quando che sia alle beati genti.

Er correr migli
or acq̃ alza leuele
omai lanauicella
delmio ingegno.
che lascia dietro
a se mar si cru/
dele.
Et cantero diq̃l
secondo regno.
doue lumano spi
rito si purga ⁊ disalire alciel di/
uenta degno.
Ma qui lamorta poesi risurga
o sancte muse poi che vostro sono
⁊ qui Caliope alquanto surga
Seguitãdo ilmio cãto cõq̃l sono
di cui lepiche misere sentiro
locolpo tal che disperar pdono
Dolce color doriental zaffiro
che saccoglieua nelsereno aspecto
dalmezzo puro isin alprimo giro
gliocchi miei ricomincio ildilecto
... chio usci fuor dellaura morta
che mauea cõtristati gliocchi elpecto
... pianeta che adamar cõforta
... ridere loriente
... chelli cherano insua scorta
... aman dextra ⁊ puosi mente
... polo ⁊ vidi quattro stelle
... mai fuor che allaprima gente
... parea ilciel diloz fiammelle
... settentrionale vedouo sito
... priuato se dimirar quelle
... diloro ilguardo fui partito
... me uolgendo allaltro polo
... ilcarro gia cra sparito
... dime un ueglio solo
... reuerenza in uista
che piu nõ dee apadre alcun figliuolo
L ungha labarba ⁊ dipel bianco mista
portaua isuo capelli simigliante
dequai cadeua alpetto doppia lista
L iraggi delle quattro luci sancte
fregiauan si lasua faccia dilume
chio ilvedea comel sol fosse dauante
C hi siete voi che contro alcieco fiume
fuggita auete laprigione ecterna?
dissel mouendo quelle honeste piume
C hi ua guidati o chi ui fu lucerna
uscendo fuor delaprofonda nocte
che sempre nera fa lavalle inferna?
S on leleggi dabisso cosi rotte
oe murato ilciel nuouo consiglio
che dannati venite alle mie grotte?
L oduca mio allor midie dipiglio
et cõ parole ⁊ cõ mani ⁊ cõ cenni
reuerenti mise legambe eleiglio
P oscia rispuose allui dame nõ venni
donna scese daciel plicui prieghi
dalla mia cõpagnia costui souenni
M a dache tuo voler che piu sispieghi
dinostra condiction comella e vera
esser non puote ilmio chatte siniegbi
Q uesti nõ uide mai lultima sera
ma p lasua follia lesu si presso
che molto poco tempo auolger era
S icomio dissi fu mandato adesso
perlui campare ⁊ non vera altra uia
che questa plaqual io misson messo
M ostrato lui tucta lagente ria
⁊ ora intendo mostrar quelli spirti
che purgan sesecto latua balia
C omio lo tratto saria lungo adirti
dellalto scende virtu che maiuta
condurlo auederti ⁊ audirti
O r tipiaccia gradir lasua venuta
liberta ua cercando che si cara
come sa chi perlei vita rifiuta
T usai che nonti fu plei amara
in vticha lamorte oue lasciasti
lauesta chalgran di sara si chiara
N on son ledicti ecterni pnoi guasti
che questi viue. ⁊ minos me non lega
ma son del cerchio oue son gliocchi casti
D i martia tua chenuista ancor tipriega

m 2

Fig. 8. *Purgatorio* 1, Speyer, 1477, ARCH.FOL.IT.1477, (f. m2r)

The start of *Purgatorio* makes this particularly clear as the blank space follows the contours of the letter 'P'. This was the first edition that we examined with Wuon-Gean and, watching her slowly turn the pages, my attention was drawn to aspects of the physical book that I had overlooked in my interest in the printed surface of the page, including the beauty of the thick paper and the elegant execution of the textblock. When Wuon-Gean and I experimented with setting moveable type in the Bodleian Bibliographical Press, I gained a new appreciation of the skill and craftsmanship that it took to produce a single line of text, having to locate each letter and place them (backwards!) in the order that will allow them to print correctly on the page.

As you might imagine, it was technologically difficult and therefore expensive and time consuming to reproduce illustrations alongside text in the early era of printing. Dante's *Comedy* did, however, receive a full visual treatment by the early 1490s, just under 20 years after the first copy of the poem was released in print. The second oldest edition in the Taylor reflects these developments. Printed in Venice in March 1491, this large folio format book encourages the viewer to enter into the journey of the text, announcing the start of the poem with a full-page woodcut placed inside an elaborate frame (fig. 2). A series of vignettes unfold within this single image as Dante (helpfully labelled for the viewer) emerges despondently from a dark wood and looks up to the top of a mountain from the forest's edge before turning back, hands raised in dismay, as three wild beasts pursue him down the slope towards a second figure (Virgilio) who walks towards him, pointing out the way. These events follow the narrative recounted in Dante's poem, focusing on the action of the plot (in which Dante describes himself emerging from a 'selva oscura', or dark wood) rather than on the metaphors used to describe his experience (which he compares to a shipwreck).

This edition is the first to present a printed illustration for every canto of the text. Only three of these woodcuts are full-page (the images at the start of *Inferno*, *Purgatorio*, and *Paradiso*). The remaining 97 images are smaller and more square. They sit just above the poem at the start of each canto, summarising its main action and labelling the figures as they move through the different realms. We spent a lot of time with this edition during the 'Looking for Dante' project and most of our discussions about the content of the poem – the episodes in the text and the characters that Dante encounters – were sparked by these illustrations. They appear obliquely in Wuon-Gean's new series of prints, remembered in the jumbled forms of suffering bodies and the depth of the landscapes inked on the page.

Hot on the heels of this historical book, another Venetian printshop released an illustrated Dante with almost identical layout and images, printed by Pietro di Piasi only eight months later, in November 1491. Dispensing with full-page woodcuts, the November edition contains 100 small, square illustrations placed at the start of each canto. These images follow the iconography of the earlier edition so closely that it often is hard to tell them apart, although they do show some differences. As well as being slightly larger, the November illustrations are finer and more detailed, as we can see in the case of *Inferno* 5, which includes a second figural group next to Dante and Virgil in the centre of the lower half of the composition (figs. 9 & 10). These woodblocks were used again in an edition printed in Venice in 1497 by Pietro Quarengi, and it is in this edition that we have consulted them. These books represent a veritable trend in recycling imagery both in physical terms (using the same woodblocks) and in pictorial practices (replicating the imagery employed in other people's illustrations), a visual trace of the economic and artisanal exchanges that took place in the busy world of Venetian printing in this dynamic moment of technological innovation.

Some early print editions of the *Comedy* did offer iconographic innovations. In 1512 a slightly smaller, quarto-size book was printed in Venice by Bernardino Stagnino da Trino with an entirely new set of illustrations which follow the key elements of the older compositions but can be clearly distinguished by their use of shading. In the illustration for *Inferno* 5, for example, when Dante and Virgil enter the realm of the lustful, these woodcuts make use of the two-tier composition present in earlier illustrations to create a kinetic narrative shift that signals the arrival of some of the poem's most famous and contentious figures, Francesca and her lover Paolo (fig. 11).

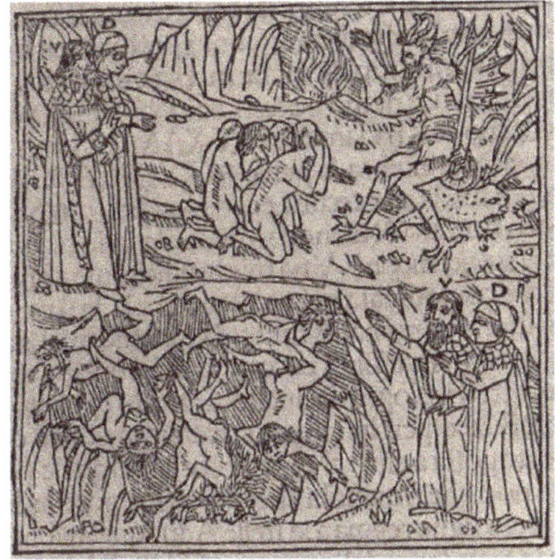

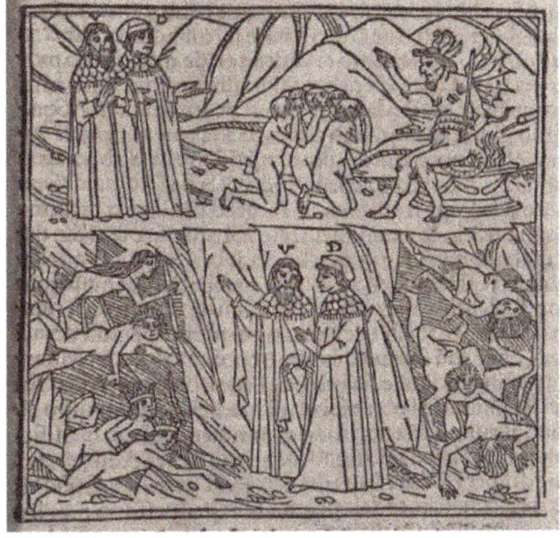

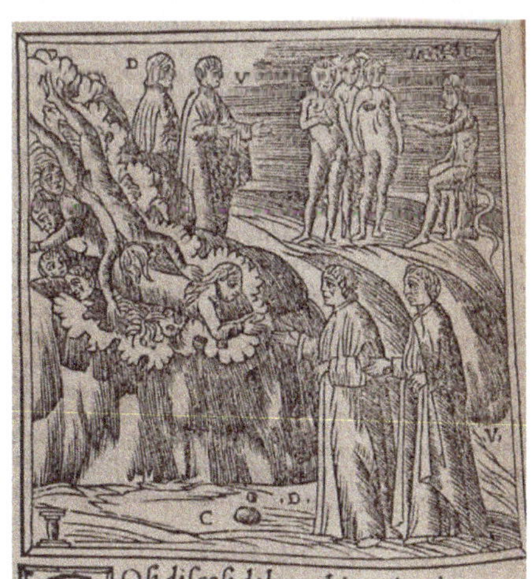

Tumbling upon each other in a close combination of limbs, this collection of human forms and cloudlike swirls presents a dynamism that is not present in the earlier illustrations. The encounter between Dante and Francesca is also much closer: Dante's open palm, a small gesture in the earlier blocks, is matched by a corresponding gesture in the Stagnino print as Francesca's outstretched hand stops only inches away. Aspects of this tangled iconography can be noted in the falling forms that appear in some of Wuon-Gean's prints, including the embrace depicted in *Am-Or / Am-More*, although this response to the story of Francesca and Paolo captures the lovers in a more peaceful moment.

The print in Stagnino's edition for *Inferno* 26, the canto in which Dante encounters the Greek hero Ulisse (Ulysses) trapped inside a tongue of flame, displays a similar intensification in narrative focus.

From top: Fig. 9. *Inferno* 5, Codecà, 1491, ARCH.FOL.IT.1491(1), (f. d8r)

Fig. 10. *Inferno* 5, Quarengi, 1497, ARCH.FOL.IT.1497(1), (f. d7r)

Fig. 11. *Inferno* 5, Stagnino, 1512, ARCH.8o.IT.1512, (f. f3v)

In the realm of the fraudulent, when Dante begs to converse with the enflamed sinners, his guide Virgil actually tells him to be silent, insisting that he 'do the talking' ('Lascia parlare a me', *Inferno* 26.73). The earlier illustrations capture this detail precisely, placing Virgil closer to the flames (fig. 12). In the new cuts from 1512, however, Dante (signalled by the letter D above his head) has his hands raised in a sign of conversation (fig. 13). In the drive to centre the scene on the protagonist, the woodcuts in Stagnino's edition stray from the letter of the text, leading an attentive reader to question whether these images are illustrating the poem or whether they are more interested in conversing with the visual tradition of earlier woodblock prints.

The interest in envisioning the narrative episodes in Dante's poem represents an important strand in the history of illuminating the *Comedy* in print, but it is not the only focus of the visual tradition. Alongside the figures and the fiction, makers of printed books were interested in representing the landscapes of Dante's Otherworld. As Simon Gilson discusses in his essay, writers and editors of the sixteenth century began to pay conspicuous attention to mapping Dante's *Inferno*.

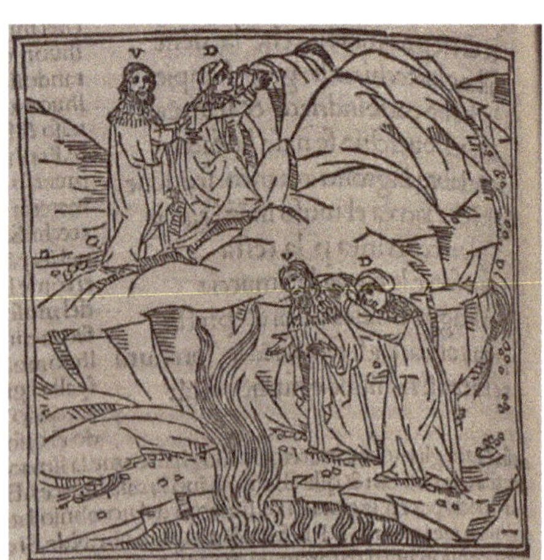

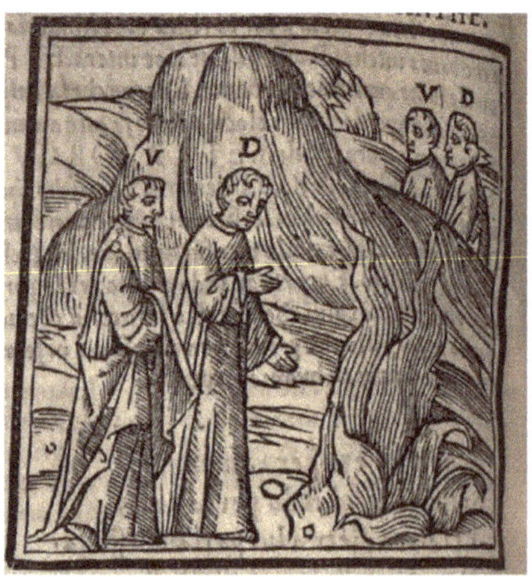

Above: Fig. 12. *Inferno* 26, Quarengi, 1497, ARCH.FOL.IT.1497(1), (f. o4v)
Fig. 13. *Inferno* 26, Stagnino, 1512, ARCH.8o.IT.1512, (f. v4v)

This trend had early beginnings. Already in the edition printed in Florence in 1481 Cristoforo Landino had dedicated an extended part of the introduction to his commentary to discussing the location, shape, and size of Hell. Here, Landino emphasises the idea that Dante describes Hell so accurately that 'con terminate misure si può comprendere' (it can be understood in relation to specific measurements). The first print publication to translate this interest into an actual map of Hell was produced by the incredibly popular publisher, Aldus Manutius, in 1515. As Simon Gilson notes, this edition includes the first full map of the *Inferno* in print and two woodcut diagrams of the sins in Hell (fig. 3) and Purgatory.

Although it does not contain a treatise on these topics, Aldus' 1515 edition is prefaced with the title: 'Dante col sito, et forma dell'Inferno tratta dalla istessa descrittione del poeta'. The map of Hell, despite its small size, is very detailed (fig. 14). The different realms and even some of the figures Dante and Virgil encounter are labelled for easy recognition (like Paolo and Francesca in the upper righthand corner of the map).

A remarkable detail in a slightly later publication on the same topic presents a striking crossover between these cartographic efforts and the real-world mapping that took place in sixteenth-century Europe. In the 1540s an Academician from Florence, Pierfrancesco Giambullari, produced a new treatise on the topic of measuring Hell, which was probably published at the author's own cost. While most of the woodcuts in this edition follow the iconography used for the maps and diagrams of *Inferno* printed in an earlier edition realised by the Giunta printshop in Florence in 1506, a new map of the world used to show the location of Hell includes an intriguing detail. In the south-western hemisphere, a large continent is labelled 'terra incognita' (fig. 4). A stock phrase for 'unknown land', this small feature may relate to the increased interest in global travel that coincided with the colonial expansionism of the sixteenth century, in which Florence played a role: Amerigio Vespucci, the navigator whose name would be given to the 'terra incognita' now known as America, was Florentine.

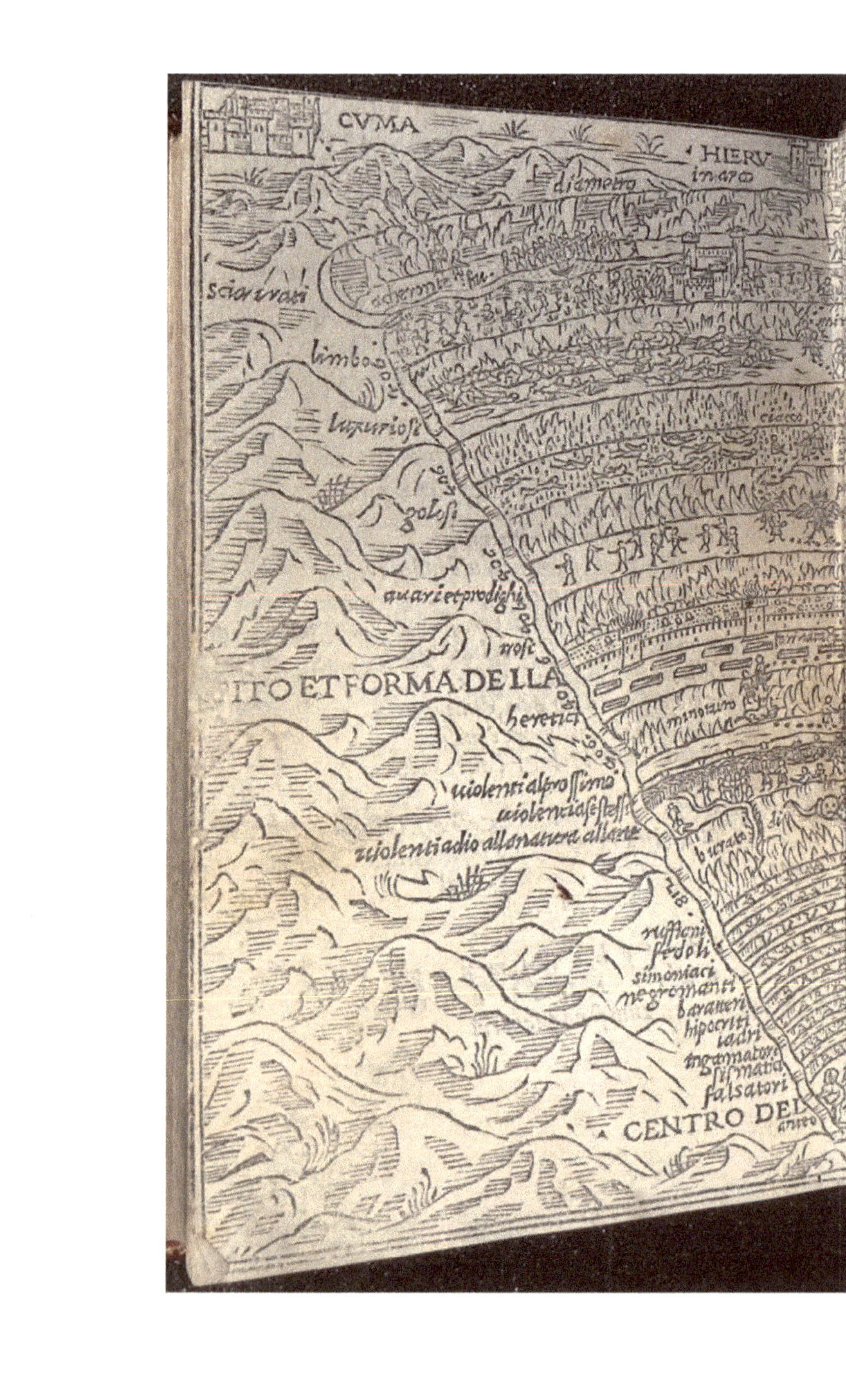

CVMA
HERV
diametro
limbo
luxuriosi
golosi
irosi
ITO ET FORMA DE LLA
heretici
uiolenti al prossimo
uiolenti a se stessi
uiolenti a dio alla natura alla arte
simoniaci
negromanti
barattieri
hipocriti
ladri
falsatori
CENTRO DEL

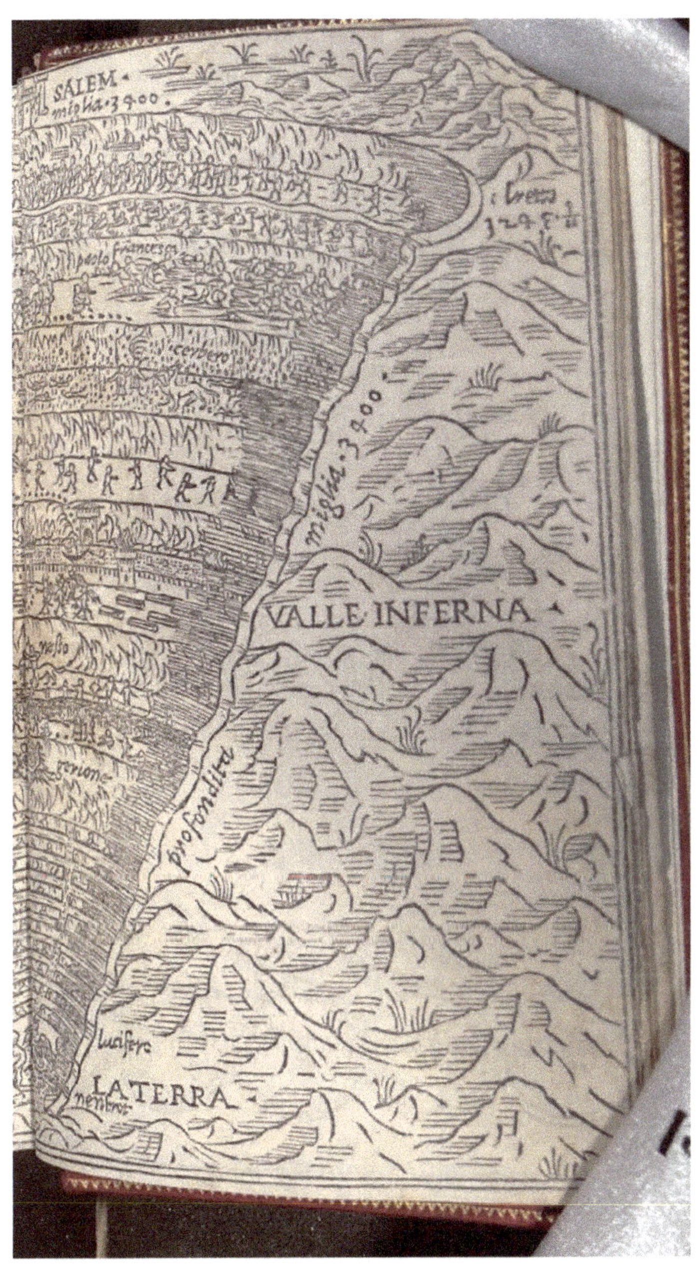

Fig. 14. Map of Hell, Aldus, 1515, ARCH.8o.IT.1515(1), (f. H5r & H5v)

In 1544, we see the publication of the first edition to seriously combine this interest in mapping Dante with the traditions of illustrating the narrative seen in earlier editions. Printed by Francesco Marcolini in Venice, this edition presents a remarkably new iconography that was the result of a professional collaboration between artisans and exegetes. Accompanying an extended 'Descrittione de lo Inferno', written by the scholar Alessandro Vellutello as part of the new commentary that he produced on Dante's poem, ten three-quarter page woodcuts illustrate the circles of Hell. These woodcuts were conceived in close relation to Vellutello's 'Nuova Esposizione'. Preparatory drawings, held in the Pierpoint Morgan Library in New York – some of which include extensive textual notes – reveal the detailed exegetical intertest behind the iconography in this volume.

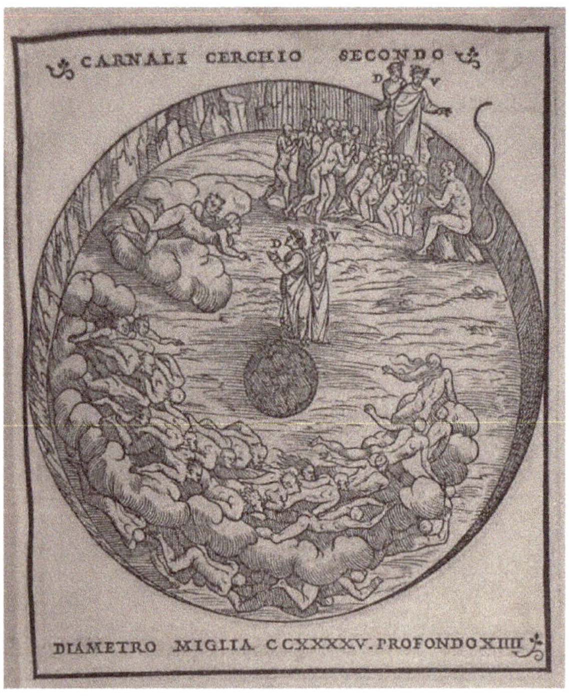

Fig. 15. Circle of Lustful, Marcolini, 1544, ARCH.8o.IT.1544 (1), (f. BB3r)

In the diagram of the circle of the lustful, for example, Dante's encounter with Francesca is rendered in a composition that is familiar from earlier illustrations (fig. 15). The visual experience, however, is visibly more dynamic as multiple figural groups are rendered in flowing lines that unite the depicted space. This reconfiguration places the scene within a circular round, lending the image a scientific tone that goes some way towards reflecting the visual logic of the cross-section used for the maps of Hell printed in other editions from this century, although the content of this image is more focused on poetic narrative than infernal topography.

Another series of woodcuts accompany the text of Dante's poem. These differ from the diagrams presented in the opening treatise, although some of their iconographic features are almost identical. The continued use of a diagrammatic visual logic to illustrate the narrative of the poem offers a new approach to the visualisation of Dante's text, integrating the increasingly cartographic interest in the poem with the older tradition of representing the main events in the plot. This fusion is achieved, as we have seen, through the use of a cross-section composition and also through the imposition of a bird's-eye view on the scene. These visual approaches manifest a sense of topographical perspective that places the viewer at a distance, allowing them to occupy a position of detached observation that is less possible in narrative illustrations, which tend to place the viewer *in media res*. In a modern sense, these circular cross-sections proffer the infernal realms like petri dishes, encouraging a particularly analytical gaze. These designs also give an impression of the extent of the human suffering envisioned in Dante's hell, filling the foreground with writhing masses of bodies that slip over into *mis-en-abyme* if we peer into the descending pit at the centre of each circle, which opens onto regions deeper in the bowels of Hell, synthesising multiple *canti* into a single space. As well as the cross-section, the Marcolini edition employs a full-frame perspective, as we can see from the illustration for *Purgatorio* 1. Here, the viewer is placed much closer to the action of the scene, emphasising the steep incline of the mountain that Dante and the purging souls must climb (fig. 16).

The success of these woodcuts is signalled by their reuse in later editions. As well as Domenico Farri's reprints of the Dolce edition (1569 and 1578), these images appear in a large format volume printed in Venice in 1564 by the Sessa printshop (fig. 5). Combining Vellutello's commentary with the earlier gloss by Cristoforo Landino and new allegorical interpretations and summaries written by the editor, Francesco Sansovino, this volume offers a complex combination of elements that weave picture and word into a new, monumental frame for Dante's text.

Reusing the woodblocks made for Marcolini's 1544 *Comedy*, this edition, and its own subsequent reprints in 1578 and 1596, amplify the visual content through careful placing on the page. The illustration for *Purgatorio* 1 is even repeated at the end of *Inferno*, showing a considered use of the woodcut as a sequencing device. It is interesting to note that the *argomento* (narrative description) and *allegoria* (allegorical interpretation) provided for this canto by the editor, Sansovino, both reflect the main narrative events present in the print: the encounter with the soul of Cato, who instructs Virgil to wash Dante's face clean of the dirt from Hell and to encircle his waist with a purifying reed. These purgatorial actions take place in the foreground, while the meeting with Cato is placed close to the base of the towering mountain. Cato, labelled with the letter C, points his finger at Virgil, signalling his specific commands. After earlier commentators, Sansovino interprets the reed as a symbol of humility and honesty ('la sincerità, & humiltà, parti necessarie a chi si vuol purgar de peccati').

This image is the only motif from the historical editions to appear directly inside Wuon-Gean's new prints. Interpreted as an embrace, the purifying rite becomes an intimate moment of connection between the artist and the book, as well as between the characters on the page. The title of this new print, *Touch In / In Touch*, highlights the event as a touchstone moment in Wuon-Gean's own encounter with Dante and offers a fitting transition from the infernal imagery of the preceding prints, replacing the stars visible at the top of this woodblock with the windows of the Taylor Institution Library.

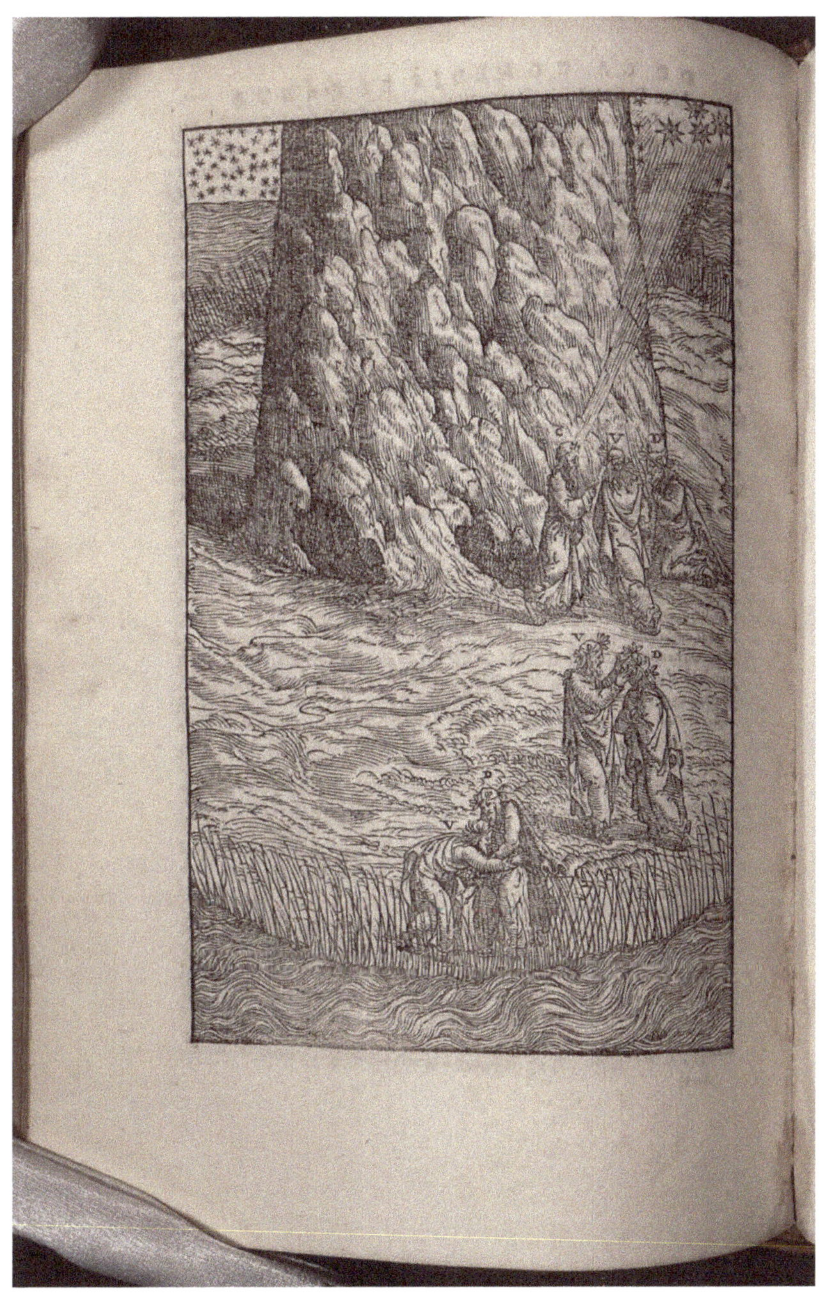

Fig. 16. *Purgatorio* 1, Marcolini, 1544, ARCH.8o.IT.1544 (1), (f. t7v)

The Marcolini woodblocks, first published in 1544, were replicated in later visual schemes. A small (12mo) edition released by the Venetian printer Gabriel Giolito in 1555 – the first edition to add the epithet 'divine' to the title of Dante's text – reconfigures their iconography in new prints placed at the start and end of each of the three *cantiche*. These blocks reduce the size of the originals and set them within elaborate, grotesque frames (fig. 17). Rather than replicating the scientific cross-section, this series only includes the narrative illustrations for the first, second, and final *canti* of *Inferno* and *Purgatorio*, plus illustrations for *Paradiso* 1 and 3, compensating for the reduction in size by zooming in on particular details.

Situating the otherworldly spaces of the *Comedy* within topographical coordinates that attempt to recreate a sense of real-world distance, these images encourage readers to visualise Dante's poetic geography on a human scale that fits within the pages of a book, a representative drive that remains powerful to this day, as Wuon-Gean's new series of prints stand to prove.

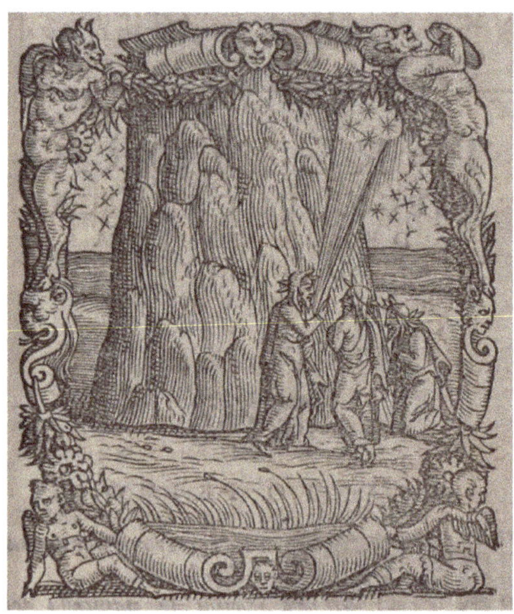

Fig. 17. *Purgatorio* 1, Giolito, 1555, (MOORE.1.A.3), (f. I5r)

List of Early Editions

i) Speyer, 1477, Venice
Taylorian shelfmark: ARCH.FOL.IT.1477

ii) Codecà, 1491, Venice
Taylorian shelfmark: ARCH.FOL.IT.1491(1)

iii) Quarengi, 1497, Venice
Taylorian shelfmark: ARCH.FOL.IT.1497(1)

iv) Stagnino, 1512, Venice
Taylorian shelfmark: ARCH.8o.IT.1512

v) Aldine, 1515, Venice
Taylorian shelfmark: ARCH.8o.IT.1515(1)

vi) Paganini, 1520?, [Toscolano]
Taylorian shelfmark: ARCH.8o.IT.1506

vii) Neri Dortelata, 1544, Florence
Taylorian shelfmark: MOORE.4.A.29

viii) Marcolini, 1544, Venice
Taylorian shelfmark: ARCH.8o.IT.1544 (1)

ix) Giolito, 1555, Venice
Taylorian shelfmark: MOORE.1.A.3

x) Sessa, 1564, Venice
Taylorian shelfmark: ARCH.FOL.IT.1564 (1)

Speyer, 1477, Venice

ARCH.FOL.IT.1477

This large folio size book is the earliest printed copy of Dante's *Commedia* in the Taylorian collections. It is also the first print edition of the *Commedia* to contain a commentary, which is misattributed in the book's colophon to Benvenuto da Imola and is actually the vernacular commentary of Iacomo della Lana. The opening initials and other section markers are left blank, perhaps to encourage hand illumination. Irregular blank spaces also appear in the middle of the text block, which probably relate to the diagrams often included alongside the commentary in manuscript versions of the text. The paratextual material includes Boccaccio's *Vita di Dante* and summaries of the three *cantiche*. Each *cantica* is preceded by further summaries of the separate *canti* and the edition closes with the pseudo-Dantean poem called the 'Credo di Dante' as well as the 'Capitoli' of Jacopo Alighieri and Bosone da Gubbio, often found together in manuscripts.

The copy in the Taylorian has brown leather binding, tooled and polished, a raised spine with gilded lettering, and marbled end paper. A Taylor Institution bookplate is glued on the upper pastedown. This plate includes a handwritten note that records the cost of the volume ('purchased for £32/10/06') and a date ('1875'). This means it was purchased after Friedrich Max Müller, the second Professor of Modern European Languages, secured funds for the expansion of the library's collection of early materials.

Further reading: Ambrogio: 34–35; Richardson: ix; Trovato: 123; Wolf: 76–77; Notre Dame

Codecà, 1491, Venice

This edition is also in a large folio format. It is the first printed *Commedia* to contain a full set of illustrations for every canto of the poem. The illustrations for the first *canti* of *Inferno*, *Purgatorio*, and *Paradiso* are all full-page woodcuts enclosed in elaborate frames. The remaining 97 illustrations are smaller, square woodcuts. The iconography is very close to that of the edition printed in Brescia in 1487, although that volume only presents one illustration for the whole *Paradiso*. The iconography of this edition is also identifiably different to that of the first illustrated *Commedia* in print, produced in Florence in 1481 (with engravings for the first 19 *canti* of *Inferno* only). Among the complex paratextual materials are sidenotes in the margin that draw attention to major figures mentioned in the commentary. These printed marginalia were important to Pietro da Figino, the *correttore* (editor) of the text, who mentions them, but not the images, in the colophon where he signs his name at the end of the edition ('& ha a[n]chora posto di fora i[n] li margini tutte le historie nota[n]de & li nomi p[ro]prii che si trovano i[n] ditta opera'). This volume was reprinted with some variations by the same printshop in 1493.

The copy in the Taylor is bounded in white animal skin and has a smooth spine and marbled end paper. It also has two bookplates on the upper pastedown. One plate belongs to the Taylor Institution and bears in pencil the date '1886'. The other plate belongs to Edward Cheney (1803–1884), a British art collector, whose crest represents a knightly helmet inside an oval frame surrounded by the motto 'fato prudentia maior'. Written on this plate, in a different pencil, is the price '£4.18.0'. After his death in 1884, many of Cheney's books were sold off at two auctions held by two Sotheby's (in 1885 and 1886). Like others of Cheney's books, this copy has a handwritten note on the first fly leaf recording the details of his acquisition: 'E. C. / Venice / 3rd / D. / 1835'.

Further reading: Ambrogio: 40–41; Gilson: 27–31; Trovato: 133; Wolf: 87–89; Notre Dame

Quarengi, 1497, Venice

ARCH.FOL.IT.1497(1)

Printed in Venice in 1497, this edition copies elements in the earlier books printed by Codecà in 1491 and in 1493. It is in a large folio format and reuses the same full-page woodcuts first printed by Codecà in 1491. The first page of *Inferno* is enclosed in a second, elaborate frame. This same frame is used in Codecà's earlier 1493 edition of the *Commedia.* Quarengi's edition also replicates the textual materials in Codecà's 1493 *Commedia*, some of its setting is even identical down to the letter, a rare phenomenon. In a variation on its predecessor, Quarengi's edition employs a different set of small woodcuts to illustrate the start of each canto, utilising the blocks made for another edition of the poem that was also printed in Venice, but six months later, in November 1491, by Pietro di Piasi. These blocks closely follow the iconographic elements of Codecà's illustrations as well as those in the edition printed in Brescia in 1487. Larger and more detailed, these illustrations are generally finer in style than those in Codecà's edition. Both sets of blocks continued to be reused in different combinations between multiple Venetian printshops well into the sixteenth century.

The Taylorian copy has brown leather binding that is tooled and polished. It has a Taylor Institution bookplate with the date 1889 written in purple pencil. In the same purple pencil, a handwritten note records the price and provenance of the purchase: '£10 / purchased from | Messers J. Parker | Oxford, 1889'. The Parker bookshop was at 27 Broad Street, the location of Blackwell's Art & Poster Shop today. Parker's business operated at that site from 1816 until it was taken over by Blackwell's in the 1990s.

Further reading: Ambrogio: 42; Gilson: 31; Richardson: 29; Notre Dame

Stagnino, 1512, Venice

ARCH.8o.IT.1512

This mid-size, quarto volume continues the tradition of the large Venetian Dantes, with some innovations. The title page uses a striking combination of black and red ink as well as an eye-catching printer's device to signal the role of the printshop in the production of the volume. It reproduces the text of Dante's poem edited by Pietro Bembo and first printed in 1502 by the famous Venetian printer Aldus Manutius. It also offers Pietro da Figino's edition of Landino's commentary but, in the colophon at the end of the volume, signals that revisions have been made by a new group of unnamed editors: 'etia[m] noviter per altri excellenti huo[m]i[ni]' (now recently [revised] by other excellent men). This edition also contains a new series of illustrations: one full-page woodcut for the start of the *Inferno* and 99 small woodcuts to mark the beginning of all the other *canti*. These new blocks offer a fresh iconography that combines the patterns set in the 1491 editions with identifiably strong linear shading. This edition met with success and was reprinted twice over the next decades in an almost identical setting (save for the addition of some missing page numbers).

The copy in the Taylor has dark brown, tooled leather binding and a smooth spine. Visible holes in the middle of the top edges and along the side edge show that the book used to have clasps. The copy has extensive marginal notes in black ink, written in Latin with scribal abbreviations. An autograph in the same hand identifying the owner as a 'ci. Fiorenti' (citizen of Florence) is present on the title page.

Further reading: Ambrogio: 52; Gilson: 43; Trovato: 158; Wolf: 90–93; Notre Dame

Aldine, 1515, Venice

ARCH.8o.IT.1515(1); MOORE.1.A.2)

This small octavo edition is the second *Commedia* printed by Aldus Manutius, a famous Venetian printer, who released his first edition of Dante's poem in 1502 with text edited by Pietro Bembo, a Venetian academic who spoke and wrote about Dante in heated discussions of national identity and the politics of language, advocating for and establishing a national literature in a time of war and fragmentation. Aldus' editions were frequently counterfeited by other printers. This edition contains some corrections to the earlier text and bears a new title ('Dante col sito, et forma dell'Inferno tratta dalla istessa descrittione del poeta') and new illustrations of the topography of *Inferno* and the organisation of the sins in Hell and Purgatory. The map, a detailed cross-section of the circles of Hell, includes miniature representations of the pilgrim's journey in which key episodes and encounters with specific figures are labelled for easy recognition. The edition opens with a letter to the poet Vittoria Colonna and closes with a colophon that names the printers as Aldus and Andrea da Asola, the printer's father-in-law.

The Taylorian edition at ARCH.8o.IT.1515(1) has red leather binding with gold details and some raising on the spine. As well as marbled flypaper, the copy displays a Taylor Institution bookplate. On the verso of the front flyleaf, a note in pencil reads: 'from Dr Scartazzini's | Library, Nov. 1884 | (120 francs) | from U. Hoepli, Milano | Catal. No 21'. Dr Scartazzini was a respected literary critic who produced an edition of and commentary on the *Commedia* in four volumes, published between 1874–1890. Scartazzini also edited the first two volumes of the *Enciclopedia dantesca*, published between 1896–1899 by Ulrico Hoepli in Milan.

Further reading Ambrogio: 52–53; Gilson: 43–45; Mecca: 25–33; Richardson: 58; Notre Dame

Paganini, 1520?, [Toscolano]

ARCH.8o.IT.1506

This small format edition, of uncertain date, is essentially an elegant octavo that follows the model of the 1515 Aldine (prepared by Bembo), presenting the text in italic type in a single column and with running headers for each canticle. Like Manutius' edition, this edition has two title pages reading: 'Dante col sito, et forma dell'Inferno' and 'Lo'nferno e'l Purgatorio e'l Paradiso di Dante Alaghieri'. This edition is also very close to another copycat Aldine printed in Venice in 1515 by the printer Gregorio de Gregoriis. It concludes with a two-page map of Hell with considerable and intricate detail and two diagrammatic representations of the ordering of sins in *Inferno* and of capital vices in *Purgatorio.* All three of these illustrative paratexts present a rather crude recutting of the main elements present in Gregoriis' images as well as the original Aldine. It is thought to have been printed between 1527 and 1533 in the city of Toscolano, a key location for the production of paper in Northern Italy. Paganini had produced another, smaller (24mo) edition with the same textual materials in 1515 which includes another set of (smaller) woodcuts, again based most closely on those in Gregoriis' counterfeit.

The Taylorian edition is bound in white animal skin with red and gold lettering and decoration. The front and back covers elegantly replicate the title page and printer's device present inside the book. This copy has a Taylor Institution bookplate on the upper pastedown. On the verso of the first leaf an owner's mark, probably a name, is partially visible despite attempts at erasure, at bottom of the page.

Further reading: Ambrogio: 55; Gilson: 45;
Mecca: 25–33; Notre Dame

Neri Dortelata, 1544, Florence

MOORE.4.A.29 and 101.C.14

Printed in Florence, rather than Venice, this edition reflects the particular scholarly and linguistic interests of the Florentine intelligentsia. Closely inspired by an earlier Florentine edition printed by Lucantonio Giunta in 1506, this is a volume about Dante rather than a volume containing Dante's poem. In a small, octavo format, this book publishes a new treatise on measurements in *Inferno* whose author includes his name in the title: 'Pierfrancesco Giambullari accademico fior. De 'l sito, forma, & misure, dello Inferno di Dante'. Although the topic is present in the editions that reprint Landino's commentary, this is the first edition since Giunta's 1506 publication to engage with the topic of the topography of Hell in written format. Probably self-published, this volume reflects the beliefs and interests of Giambullari, a Florentine scholar who gave public lectures on Dante at the Accademia Fiorentina and centred several linguistic-political theories on Dante's writings. Following the pattern presented in the 1506 edition, this volume contains woodcuts that present a scientific view of Dante's poetic landscapes, including mathematical diagrams and a new cross-section of the bottom of hell. This edition also contains a map of the world that labels a large continent in the Western hemisphere as 'terra incognita', a potential reflection of Florentine interest in the European colonial expansionism of the sixteenth century.

The copy at MOORE.4.A.29 is bound in a hard red cloth cover. It has a Queen's College bookplate on the upper pasteboard, announcing it was loaned to the Taylorian, and a Moore Collection bookplate on first flyleaf. Edward Moore (1835–1916) was a renowned Dante scholar who worked at Oxford for many years and, in 1876, founded the Oxford Dante Society. His books were bequeathed to Queen's college and then placed on loan to the Taylor Library in 1939. On the second flyleaf, a hand written note displays the date 'May 1887'. Tipped in to the title page on the long lefthand edge is a typed note that reads: 'Dell'Abate Carlo Talenti'. Talenti was an eighteenth-century historian who actively engaged with local history and wrote an accurate account of the siege of the city of Brescello (at the northern edge of the Italian province of Reggio Emilia) which was sacked by Franco-Spanish forces in 1702.

Marcolini, 1544, Venice

ARCH.8o.IT.1544 (1); ARCH.8o.IT.1544 (2)

This edition is a larger, quarto size volume published in Venice. It presents an important intervention into the tradition of editing and reading Dante's text. As well as promoting a new commentary by the Venetian academic Alessandro Vellutello this edition publishes a new series of woodcuts which diverge almost entirely from the preceding iconographic traditions. Combining the interest in mapping Hell with the desire for a visual accompaniment to the narrative journey of the text, these woodblocks follow the cartographic visual style — already firmly associated with illustrations of the *Commedia* in print — and combine it with a sensitive close reading of the poem. As well as a dedication and a letter from Vellutello to the readers, the edition contains a new life of the poet and an extended 'Descrittione de lo Inferno', accompanied by ten three-quarter page woodcuts illustrating the circles of Hell. The poem is accompanied by another, newer set of illustrations which follow the pattern established in the early Venetian editions by presenting three full-page woodcuts at the start of each cantica. These draw on the iconographic elements of the earlier tradition but render them in a more naturalist style. The edition also contains a large series of three-quarter page illustrations that accompany almost every canto, mixing narrative scenes with topographical bird's-eye views in a truly new vision of Dante's text.

The Taylorian copy at ARCH.8o.IT.1544 (1) has brown leather binding with raising on the spine and visible marks left by clasps on the long edge. The binding is gilded in parts, although much of this decoration is now lost. An autograph is present on the title page.

Further reading: Ambrogio: 57–58; Gilson: 178–194; Mecca: 47–56; Wolf: 97–99; Notre Dame

Giolito, 1555, Venice

MOORE.1.A.3

This small 12° edition is the first to add the word 'divine' to the title of Dante's poem, an epithet that has remained popular to this day. It includes several new paratexts by Ludovico Dolce, one of the most representative of the so-called polygraphs, indefatigable vernacular writers and producers of copy for the Venetian printing presses. As well as new marginal notes, Dolce's edition offers summaries and allegorical interpretations of each canto and a glossary of complex terms (Dante's poem was now more than 200 years-old). The edition also contains a new set of woodcuts that follow the iconography of Marcolini's 1544 edition but reduce the scenes for the smaller format. The edition opens with a dedicatory letter to the Bishop of San Marco (Coriolano Martirano) and a table for locating the marginal notes. A portrait of Dante is included after the dedicatory letter, which encloses the distinctly classicised poet in a medallion (a motif present in an earlier edition from 1536 also printed by the Giolito family printshop). A poem attributed to Boccaccio accompanies this image, around which is written the phrase 'Il divino poeta Dante'. These different paratextual elements are signalled in the long title and separated by numerous printer's ornaments. The edition was reprinted by Domenico Frarri in 1569 and 1578.

This edition is bound in white animal skin. It has the bookplates of Queen's College and the Moore Collection. A note on the upperpaste board signed by Moore, reads: 'this is I believe the first edition in which the epithetic "Divina Comedia" is found| EM'. This observation has been crossed out by a later, unsigned, hand with the reply: 'No. It is in 1516'. The claim is backed up with a reference to Paul Colomb de Batines' 1845 *Bibliografia dantesca*, a work that incorrectly records the title of Stagnino's 1516 edition as 'La divina comedia col comento di Christoforo Landino'. Surviving copies show that the 1516 edition was actually entitled 'Opere del Divino Poeta Danthe con suoi comenti' (see ARCH.8o.IT.1512), providing Moore right.

Further reading: Ambrogio: 62–63; Gilson: 225–233; Richardson: 117; Notre Dame

Sessa, 1564, Venice

ARCH.FOL.IT.1564 (1–3)

Impressive in both size and content, this large, folio book presents an unprecedented combination of earlier textual traditions, printing the poem alongside two of its commentaries: Landino's *Comento* and Vellutello's *Nuova espositione*. The editor behind this ambitious programme, Francesco Sansovino, included several additions to Landino's prologue and indicated his name (Sanv.) next to new '*allegorie*' (short, allegorical interpretations) that are placed at the start of each canto. The text is glossed with short *argomenti* that are not attributed to a particular author but that closely follow the paratexts included in Ludovico Dolce's edition, printed by Giolito in Venice in 1555. Accompanying the poem are reprints of the woodblocks used by Marcolini in 1544. A new portrait of Dante appears on the title page, enclosed in an elaborate frame, in which the poet's features retain the classicizing cast seen in the portrait in Giolito's 1555 edition but are softened into an almost wistful look as Dante's face is angled away from the viewer and he gazes off into the distance.

The copy at ARCH.FOL.IT.1564 (1) has embossed brown leather binding and marbled paper on the pastedowns. It holds the bookplates of Robert Finch (1783–1830), an antiquarian who lived in Rome and bequeathed his books to the University of Oxford. Finch's library, along with the books of Sir Robert Taylor, was the first collection to arrive at the Taylor Institution when it opened in 1847.

Further reading: Ambrogio: 64; Wolf: 100–102; Gilson: 233–239; Richardson: 144–145; Notre Dame

Further Reading

Ambrogio = *Dante poeta e italiano. Legato con amore in un volume. Mostra di manoscritti e stampe antiche della raccolta di Livio Ambrogio. Roma, Palazzo Incontro, 21 giugno-31 luglio 2011*, ed. Livio Ambrogio, Chiara Concina, Enrico Malato, and Andrea Mazzucchi (Salerno Editrice: Rome, 2011).

Gilson = Simon Gilson, *Reading Dante in Renaissance Italy: Florence, Venice, and the "Divine Poet"* (Cambridge: Cambridge University Press, 2018).

Mecca = Angelo Eugenio Mecca, 'La tradizione a stampa della *Commedia*: Dall'Aldina del Bembo (1502) all'edizione della Crusca (1595)', *Nuova Rivista di Letteratura Italiana* 16.1–2 (2013): 9–59.

Notre Dame = Renaissance Dante in Print (1472-1629), online exhibition https://www3.nd.edu/~italnet/Dante/

Richardson = Brian Richardson, *Print Culture in Renaissance Italy: The Editor and the Vernacular Text, 1470-1600* (Cambridge: Cambridge University Press, 1994).

Trovato = Paolo Trovato, *Con ogni diligenza corretto. La stampa e le revisioni editoriali dei testi letterari italiani (1470-1570)* (Ferrara: unifepress, 2009).

Wolf = Lucia Alma Wolf, 'Crossing Borders with the Divine Comedy: A Catalog of Selected Works from the Library of Congress', in *The Unexpected Dante: Perspectives on the Divine Comedy*, ed. Lucia Alma Wolf (Bucknell University Press, 2021), pp. 76–154

Contributors

Wuon-Gean Ho has a BA in History of Art, a professional licence as a Veterinary surgeon from Cambridge University, and an MA in Printmaking from the Royal College of Art. She has studied woodblock printmaking in Japan and been an etching fellow at the Royal Academy Schools in London. She exhibits her prints, books, and animations internationally. Her most recent solo shows were in Hong Kong, China (2023) and Buffalo, USA (2024). https://www.wuongean.com

Rebecca Bowen is a postdoctoral research associate at the University of Oxford, where she received her PhD in Italian Studies. She is also an associate scholar at the Kunsthistorisches Institut in Florenz–Max-Planck-Institut. She works on text-image relations, the writings of Dante and other medieval Italian poets, and representations of love.

Simon Gilson FBA is Agnelli-Serena Professor of Italian at the University of Oxford and a Fellow of Magdalen College. He is the author of *Reading Dante in Renaissance Italy: Florence, Venice and the Divine Poet* (2018) and other publications in Dante Studies. He has been involved in several collaborative funded research projects in the fields of medieval and Renaissance studies.